The Nevada State Constitution

Reference Guides to the State Constitutions
of the United States
G. Alan Tarr, Series Editor

This series includes a separate volume for each state constitution, analyzing its history and current status, providing a text of the constitution with a clause-by-clause commentary, a bibliography, a table of cases, and an index. A volume describing common themes and variations in state constitutional development and a final index volume to the preceding volumes are forthcoming. The following is a listing of those titles in the series that have been published to date:

Arizona
  John D. Leshy
Arkansas
  Kay Collett Goss
California
  Joseph R. Grodin, Calvin R. Massey, and
  Richard B. Cunningham
Connecticut
  Wesley W. Horton
Florida
  Talbot D'Alemberte
Hawaii
  Anne Feder Lee
Kansas
  Francis H. Heller
Louisiana
  Lee Hargrave
Maine
  Marshall J. Tinkle

Mississippi
  John W. Winkle III
Nebraska
  Robert D. Miewald and Peter J. Longo
Nevada
  Michael W. Bowers
New Jersey
  Robert F. Williams
New York
  Peter J. Galie
North Carolina
  John V. Orth
Tennessee
  Lewis L. Laska
Vermont
  William C. Hill
Wyoming
  Robert B. Keiter and Tim Newcomb

THE NEVADA STATE CONSTITUTION

A Reference Guide

Michael W. Bowers

Foreword by Frankie Sue Del Papa

KFN
1001
1864
.A6
B69
1993
West

REFERENCE GUIDES TO THE STATE CONSTITUTIONS OF THE UNITED STATES,
NUMBER 18
G. ALAN TARR, *Series Editor*

GREENWOOD PRESS
Westport, Connecticut • London

Library of Congress Cataloging-in-Publication Data

Bowers, Michael Wayne.
    The Nevada state constitution : a reference guide / Michael W.
Bowers.
        p.   cm.—(Reference guides to the state constitutions of the
United States ; no. 18)
    Includes bibliographical references and index.
    ISBN 0–313–27977–2 (alk. paper)
    1. Nevada—Constitution.   I. Nevada. Constitution. 1993.
II. Title. III. Series.
    KFN1001 1864.A6B69   1993
    342.793′023—dc20
    [347.930223]   93–20347

British Library Cataloguing in Publication Data is available.

Library of Congress Catalog Card Number: 93–20347
ISBN: 0–313–27977–2

First published in 1993

Greenwood Press, 88 Post Road West, Westport, CT 06881
An imprint of Greenwood Publishing Group, Inc.

Printed in the United States of America

The paper used in this book complies with the
Permanent Paper Standard issued by the National
Information Standards Organization (Z39.48–1984).

10 9 8 7 6 5 4 3 2 1

To the two women to whom I owe the most: my mother, Wanda Whittaker, and my grandmother, Floy Kerbo.

Contents

Contents   ix

Series Foreword

In 1776, following the declaration of independence from England, the former colonies began to draft their own constitutions. Their handiwork attracted widespread interest, and draft constitutions circulated up and down the Atlantic seaboard as constitution makers sought to benefit from the insights of their counterparts in other states. In Europe, the new constitutions found a ready audience seeking enlightenment from the American experiments in self-government. Even the delegates to the Constitutional Convention of 1787, despite their reservations about the course of political developments in the states during the decade after independence, found much that was useful in the newly adopted constitutions. And when James Madison, fulfilling a pledge given during the ratification debates, drafted the federal Bill of Rights, he found his model in the famous Declaration of Rights of the Virginia Constitution.

By the 1900s, however, few people would have looked to state constitutions for enlightenment on fundamental rights or important principles. Instead, a familiar litany of complaints was heard whenever state constitutions were mentioned. State constitutions were too long and too detailed, combining basic principles with policy prescriptions and prohibitions that had no place in the fundamental law of a state. By including such provisions, it was argued, state constitutions deprived state governments of the flexibility they needed to respond effectively to changing circumstances. This—among other factors—encouraged political reformers to look to the federal government, which was not plagued by such constitutional constraints, thereby shifting the locus of political initiative away from the states. Meanwhile, civil libertarians concluded that state bills of rights, at least as interpreted by state courts, did not adequately protect rights and therefore looked to the federal courts and the federal Bill of Rights for redress. As power and responsibility shifted from the states to Washington, so too did the attention of scholars, the legal community, and the general public.

During the early 1970s, however, state constitutions were rediscovered. The immediate impetus for this rediscovery was former President Richard Nixon's appointment of Warren Burger to succeed Earl Warren as chief justice of the U.S. Supreme Court. To civil libertarians, this appointment seemed to signal a decisive shift in the Supreme Court's jurisprudence because Burger was expected to lead the Court away from the liberal activism that had characterized the Warren Court. They therefore sought ways to safeguard the gains they had achieved for defendants, racial minorities, and the poor during Warren's tenure from erosion by the Burger Court. In particular, they began to look to state bills of rights to secure the rights of defendants and to support other civil liberties claims that they advanced in state courts.

The new judicial federalism, as it came to be called, quickly advanced beyond its initial concern to evade the mandates of the Burger Court. Indeed, less than two decades after it originated, it has become a nationwide phenomenon. For when judges and scholars turned their attention to state constitutions, they discovered an unsuspected richness. They found not only provisions that paralleled the federal Bill of Rights but also constitutional guarantees of the right to privacy and of gender equality, for example, that had no analogue in the U.S. Constitution. Careful examination of the text and history of state guarantees revealed important differences between even those provisions that most resembled federal guarantees and their federal counterparts. Looking beyond state declarations of rights, jurists and scholars discovered affirmative constitutional mandates to state governments to address such important policy concerns as education and housing. Taken altogether, these discoveries underlined the importance for the legal community of developing a better understanding of state constitutions.

The renewed interest in state constitutions has not been limited to judges and lawyers, however. State constitutional reformers have renewed their efforts with notable success: Since 1960, ten states have adopted new constitutions, and several others have undertaken major constitutional revisions. These changes have usually resulted in more streamlined constitutions and more effective state governments. Also, in recent years political activists on both the left and the right have pursued their goals through state constitutional amendments, often enacted through the initiative process, under which policy proposals can be placed directly on the ballot for voters to endorse or reject. Scholars, too, have begun to rediscover how state constitutional history can illuminate changes in political thought and practice, providing a basis for theories about the dynamics of political change in America.

Michael Bowers's excellent study of the Nevada Constitution, part of the Reference Guides to the State Constitutions of the United States series, reflects this renewed interest in state constitutions and will contribute to our knowledge about them. Because the constitutional tradition of each state is distinctive, Bowers's volume begins by tracing the history and development of the Nevada

Constitution. It then provides the complete text of Nevada's current constitution, with most sections accompanied by commentary that explains the provision and traces its origins and its interpretation by the courts and by other governmental bodies. For readers with a particular interest in a specific aspect of Nevada's constitutional experience, the book offers a bibliographical essay that discusses the most important sources dealing with the constitutional history and constitutional law of the state. Finally, the book concludes with a table of cases cited in the history and the constitutional commentary, as well as a subject index.

G. Alan Tarr

Foreword

The Nevada Constitution is one of the oldest and most durable founding documents of its kind in the West. Most other states in the region have basic governmental documents that are younger or have been more radically amended over the decades. Like the Nevada desert, this constitution has both stunning vistas and subtle, yet enduring, landscapes.

The core of the constitution, written in 1864, is intact, even though it has been amended more than 100 times. Many of the original restrictions and limitations that the original authors placed upon their elected officials continue to operate, and many of the political rights enunciated have been expanded (i.e., the rights of minorities; of women; for recall, referendum, and initiative, for apportionment, and so forth). The careful reader will find here echoes of the conflicts of the Civil War that formed the context for the original document.

It is easy, however, to also identify the provisions that were drafted to meet the needs of a predominantly mining-oriented society. Our legislative, executive, and judicial branches still must conduct much of their business within the framework established by those men who worked so hastily—encouraged by Abraham Lincoln—to get their document approved in time for the presidential election of 1864.

There were only about 40,000 people in the Territory (soon to be the State) of Nevada when this document was drafted. As this new study of the Nevada Constitution goes to press, the number of those residing in the Silver State approaches 1,300,000. Gaming and tourism have long since replaced mining and ranching as the leading enterprises, and the science and industry of the twentieth century have transformed a rugged frontier region into a laboratory for the most advanced modern technology.

Although the state is changing rapidly, the 1864 Constitution, with its amendments, is highly respected and is widely regarded as one of the most adaptable social contracts of its kind. The founders did their work well, and the people of Nevada have amended it with a keen sense of civic responsiblity.

This study will serve as a valuable tool, not only for scholars and historians, but also for anyone with a curiosity and enthusiasm for the democratic process.

Frankie Sue Del Papa, Attorney General

Acknowledgments

The publication of this book is especially pleasing to me, perhaps more than most other authors, in that it was written mostly on weekends and nights after a day of administrative duties. As with any other work of this nature, however, the debts that I owe to others are many.

Mildred Vasan, my editor at Greenwood Press, and Professor G. Alan Tarr, the series editor, patiently provided guidance on this long-awaited project. I am indebted to the staff of the Special Collections Department at the James R. Dickinson Library of the University of Nevada, Las Vegas, for their assistance in locating obscure and arcane references and works. In addition, I owe a debt of gratitude to the Nevada Humanities Committee for its award to me of a 1992 Research Fellowship so that I could pursue my research unencumbered by monetary worries. Richard Cortner of the University of Arizona and Phillip Simpson of Cameron University taught me much of what I know about political science, and for that I am truly grateful.

Finally, I thank Dean James S. Malek and the staff (Joyce Neitling, Leslie Marsh, Judy Ahlstrom, and Peter Gozelski) of the College of Liberal Arts at UNLV for their support and patience. And to Allen Svec goes a very special debt of gratitude for his advice and support during the course of writing this book.

Introduction

The constitutional history of Nevada is a short but interesting one. Unlike states to the east, Nevada does not have a colonial history and tradition, nor has it exchanged its original constitution for a modern one, as many of those states have done. In many respects, Nevada's constitution is not particularly exceptional. The Nevada Constitution has not been interpreted—as most state constitutions have not—to grant greater civil liberties protection to its citizens than the U.S. Constitution grants. It resembles other state constitutions in form and substance in providing three branches of government, a system of checks and balances, a bicameral legislature, a declaration of rights, a state militia, and so on.

In other ways, however, the constitution of Nevada and its history are as unique as the state itself. It is a state that is politically conservative, but it is also the only one to allow statewide casino gaming and legalized prostitution (by county option); a state that is 87 percent owned by the federal government; a state that prides itself on its rugged individualism but that owes much of its economic strength to the federal government's water, industrial, transportation, and military projects; a state that is the nation's seventh largest in geographical size, yet has a population of only slightly more than 1 million.

Robert F. Williams notes that the "study of a state's constitutional development can provide important insight into the broader issues of that state's political, economic, and social growth."[1] As the materials in this work attest, this is particularly true in Nevada, where the settlers agitated for independence and constitutional self-government from the first moments of their arrival in the Carson Valley. These pioneers were, in fact, so enamored of the importance of constitutional government that they wrote five "constitutions" before successfully becoming a state in 1864. This book examines Nevada's relatively short but spectacular constitutional history since 1848, and it provides an analysis of most sections of its constitution.

NOTE

1. Robert F. Williams, *The New Jersey State Constitution: A Reference Guide* (Westport, Conn.: Greenwood Press, 1990), xxi.

Part I

The Constitutional History of Nevada

BEFORE STATEHOOD

It has been suggested by at least one Nevada historian that the state's official slogan, "Battle Born," is misleading; although the state was born during the Civil War, "no Civil War battles were fought in this region, and the events that threatened the survival of the Union had little direct impact upon [the state], except politically."[1] The history of Nevada's statehood and poststatehood struggles, however, is replete with political, economic, cultural, and even quasi-military battles. Conflicts over taxation, racism, religion, and the legitimacy of the state's very existence have all affected its constitution.

The area that is now known as Nevada was ceded, along with most of the rest of the American Southwest, to the United States in 1848 by Mexico as a result of the latter's defeat in the Mexican-American War and the subsequent Treaty of Guadalupe Hidalgo. Two years later, as part of the Compromise of 1850, Congress created Utah Territory, encompassing an expansive area including all but the southern tip of present-day Nevada. From the very beginning, however, settlers in the western Utah Territory (now Nevada) sought to separate themselves from the Mormon-dominated territorial government.

Preoccupied with establishing central control in and around Salt Lake City, the territorial government led by Governor Brigham Young (who also served as the Mormons' spiritual leader) tended to ignore the westernmost portions of the territory, including the Carson Valley, which had been settled in northern Nevada in 1851 when this policy of benign neglect, the fact that many of the settlers were non-Mormons who chafed under the possibility of Mormon domination, and the lack of law and order in the area led to the creation of a squatters' government. Three meetings held in November 1851 gave rise to the adoption of "bylaws," "regulations," a council to govern the area and, interestingly, a petition to the U.S. Congress requesting the creation of "a distinct Territorial Government" for the western Utah Territory.[2] In a sense, the compact adopted by this squatters' government represents the first attempt by Nevadans to write a "constitution" and achieve independence.

In 1852 the Utah territorial government sought to establish some control over the western territory by extending its counties to the westernmost border. The attempt was, at best, half-hearted, and the continuing lack of law and order led the squatters, in 1853, to petition California for annexation "for judicial purposes until congress [sic] should otherwise provide."[3] California failed to act on the petition. Utah, fearing the loss of its territory, created Carson County in 1854. Again, however, the attempt was half-hearted, and in 1854 the residents of Carson County hired an attorney, William A. Cornwall, to write a constitution providing some form of governance for the area.

Little is known about the Cornwall constitution, and "there seems to be no evidence that it was ever presented for a vote."[4] In 1855, however, it did lead the Utah territorial government to create a third judicial district in Carson County. This time, Utah's attempts to establish authority in the area were serious; Governor Young appointed Orson Hyde, a member of the Mormon Church's Twelve Apostles, as probate and county judge to organize the area. In addition, Carson County was given a representative in the Utah Territorial Assembly. Elections were called in which all of the winning candidates but one were Mormon.

The now-realized Mormon domination of the western territory created relations between Gentiles and the Mormon government that were "of an unequivocally hostile and belligerent character" and that led to a second call by non-Mormons for annexation to California.[5] Although California responded favorably to the petition, Congress failed to act. Thus, "[b]y the middle of 1856 Carson County was organized politically, economically, and socially in the firm . . . hands of the Mormons."[6] A year later, however, Mormon control of the Carson Valley was effectively ended when Brigham Young called church members back to Salt Lake City to fend off what he believed would be an invasion of federal troops escorting President James Buchanan's newly appointed non-Mormon territorial government. That territorial government was appointed, at least in part, as a result of the federal government's belief that a new government in Utah might quell the fears of non-Mormons in the western territory. Although they ultimately were not needed in Salt Lake City, most of those who left behind their homes and farms in the western territory never returned.[7]

The Utah legislature rescinded its earlier action and made Carson County a part of Great Salt Lake County. Once again, the absence of organized government in the western territory led to a lack of law and order; in 1857 the settlers again petitioned Congress for status as a separate territory "within the shortest time possible."[8] James M. Crane, who had been elected to present the petition to Congress, predicted that it would win passage in order "to compress the limits of the Mormons and defeat their efforts to corrupt and confederate with the Indian tribes."[9] Although the bill passed the Committee on Territories in 1858, it died when the House of Representatives adjourned without taking action. Congress's failure to act appeared to be based on both the pre–Civil War strife over the territories that was gripping the country and congressional hopes that President Buchanan's newly appointed non-Mormon government would address the concerns of the western settlers.

During this period the Carson Valley was in disarray, with an ineffectual provisional government consisting of a committee of twenty-eight attempting to govern. The committee's lack of effectiveness led to the creation of a vigilante committee in 1858. It tried and sentenced several people, including at least one, ironically named "Lucky Bill" Thorrington, who was hanged for murder and cattle theft.[10] Again, Utah Territory attempted to assert its control, and the new, non-Mormon governor, Alfred Cumming, appointed Probate Judge John S. Child, who called for new elections. These elections were noted for their intense conflict and voter fraud, which was so rampant that four of the six precincts had their votes discarded. Once more, Carson County was established as a separate entity by the Utah legislature, and a territorial judge, John Cradlebaugh, was appointed.

Antagonisms between Gentiles and Mormons and lawlessness did not cease, however. In 1859 the settlers held a mass meeting to establish elections for a Washington representative and fifty delegates to an unauthorized constitutional convention. Not surprisingly, support for the convention seemed to be based less on an overwhelming desire for statehood than on a desire to be freed from the Utah Mormon government that "so [mixed] together church and state that a man [could not] obtain justice in any of its courts."[11] A nine-day convention was held later that year, presided over by Colonel John J. Musser. The constitution produced at this convention was modeled on that of California and was voted upon on September 7 concomitant to elections for a governor and legislature in the western territory.

The 1859 constitution adopted by the convention delegates provided for the "standard institutions of government, less a supreme court which was left to the discretion of the legislature." All in all, the document "reflected a faith in the democratic process, a dislike of executive power, faith in the legislative body, and a dislike of corporations."[12] The election returns were not preserved, but "there is evidence that the majority for a constitution was about four hundred, . . . although the board of canvassers failed to meet to canvass the votes, and the certificate of the president of the board, J. J. Musser, alone testified to the result."[13] Indeed, the certificate of election was, mysteriously, not issued until December 12, three months after the election.[14]

In the meantime, the Utah territorial government attempted to reestablish its control over the region by calling for elections on October 8. To protest its status under the control of Utah Territory, only three of ten precincts opened for the election, and the winning candidates refused to take office. The legislature that had been elected in the unauthorized 1859 constitutional election met in December but was forced to adjourn for lack of a quorum, although Isaac Roop "continued to assume the duties of Governor" for some time after.[15] The legislature never met again. Attempts in Washington to achieve separate territorial status also failed when the settlers' delegate, James M. Crane, died of a heart attack, and his replacement, John J. Musser, was unable to convince Congress to act.

Lawlessness was exacerbated in the western territory with the discovery, in 1859, of the Comstock Lode and the influx of treasure seekers which the discovery brought. The period between 1857 and 1861 has been characterized as the "era of anarchy and confusion," with a lack of any strong authority, law and order, or effective government.[16] A California visitor to Virginia City during this period wrote in a letter home: "I have seen more rascality, small and great, in my fairly brief forty days' sojourn to this wilderness of sagebrush, sharpers, and prostitutes, than in a thirteen years' experience in our not squeamishly moral State of California. . . . If I resided here six months I should turn out a consummate rascal."[17] Confusion reigned supreme in the summer of 1859, with three different governments in operation: "the Federal Government under [territorial district judge John] Cradlebaugh, the Utah Territorial Government's [probate] Judge Child, and the provisional government [of Isaac Roop]."[18]

In 1861, John J. Musser was finally successful in obtaining congressional passage of a bill to grant separate territorial status to the western Utah Territory. This event came about in no small part due to national politics. First, the secession of the southern states from the Union eliminated much of the opposition to territorial status, opposition based on southern beliefs that a separate territory would aid antislavery forces. Second, the influx of new residents to Nevada as a result of the discovery of the Comstock Lode led to increased population and increased pressure for separate territorial status. The territory bill was signed into law by President Buchanan on March 2, 1861.

By the time Nevada became a territory in 1861, it had already written at least three "constitutions"—the 1851 squatters' compact, the Cornwall constitution of 1854, and the 1859 constitution—but none had proved to have any efficacy or legal authority. It would be another three years and two "constitutions" later before a legitimate and successful constitution would be effected in Nevada.

NEVADA TERRITORY

President Abraham Lincoln, who took office two days after Buchanan signed the Act to Organize the Territory of Nevada, appointed the first territorial officials: James W. Nye of New York as governor and Orion Clemens of Iowa (brother of Samuel Clemens, better known as Mark Twain) as territorial secretary. Both were patronage appointments; Nye had campaigned in the West for Lincoln, and Clemens had studied law in the St. Louis offices of Lincoln's attorney general.

Confirming what Nevadans had known all along, Nye wrote in 1861 to Secretary of State William H. Seward that there was "no such thing as law or order existing in the Territory" and that a great need existed for a court system to establish mining rights.[19] Secessionist activities, a border dispute with California, and battles between the Indians and settlers exacerbated the problems Nye faced. Among the most important of the proclamations he issued to create a functioning government was the implementation of section 9 of the Territorial Act of 1861 creating a judicial system comprising a supreme court, district and probate courts, and justices of the peace. Each of the three Lincoln-appointed territorial judges was assigned to one of the three district courts, and all three sat *en banc* to form the territorial supreme court.

The territorial legislature met in 1861, 1862, and 1864 to develop a code of laws governing Nevada Territory, one quite similar to that of California and the New York code upon which it had itself been based.[20] Presaging the events that would disrupt and derail attempts to write a state constitution in later years, the legislature battled over the taxation of mines, the leading industry in the territory. Indeed, as one Nevada observer has noted, "[t]he background of Nevada politics for thirty years was a fight of mine operators against paying taxes."[21] Governor Nye sought to finance the territorial government through a tax on the gross proceeds of the mines, but the mining-dominated legislature objected and eventually passed a bill taxing only "the net profits arising from the mines."[22]

With the ink on the act granting separate territorial status barely dry, the territorial legislature in 1862 passed a measure providing for elections the following year in order to determine support for writing a state constitution and, assuming support, for the election of thirty-nine delegates to a constitutional convention. Sentiment clearly favored statehood; the ballot measure won by an overwhelming vote of 6,660 to 1,502.[23]

The Failed 1863 Constitution

The delegates meeting at the November 1863 constitutional convention, unauthorized by Congress, surely expected, given the four-to-one margin of support for statehood in the September election, that the document they wrote would be widely supported. It was not. Many issues divided the delegates over the course of their thirty-two-day convention; the issues of mine taxation and the election of state officials proved to be fatal.

That the unauthorized 1863 constitution, consisting of eighteen articles, was similar to that of California and New York is not at all surprising. "Of the 39 delegates to the Constitutional Convention, all but 5 had come from California, all but 5 were under 50 years of age, and all but 2 had been in the territory less than 5 years."[24] Additionally, New York was cited most often by the delegates as their place of birth.[25]

The 1863 constitution, which later served as a model for the successful 1864 constitution, was defeated by the voters by more than a four-to-one margin. Its defeat can be directly traced to two circumstances: the taxation of mines and a split in the territory's Union Party.

Just as the issue of mine taxation had led to conflict between Governor Nye and the 1861 legislature, so too did it create divisiveness at the 1863 convention.

One faction, led by convention president John North, supported taxing mines at the same rate as other property, arguing that "[a]ll property should bear alike the burdens of society."[26] The other faction, led by the influential mining lawyer William M. Stewart, wanted to tax only the proceeds of the mines. Stewart observed that "ninety-nine out of every one hundred prospecting experiments fail. . . . The effect of this proposition, then, is that you tax ninety-nine men who have no property in order to reach one man who has property."[27] A heavy tax on an unproductive claim, Stewart argued, "would inevitably stop the prospecting of it," thus leading to economic disaster for the fledgling state.[28] The North faction won handily at the convention and included in the constitution a provision requiring the legislature to "provide by law for a uniform and equal rate of assessment and taxation and [to] prescribe such regulations as shall secure a just valuation for taxation of all property, both real and personal including mines, and mining property."[29]

The split that occurred in the territory's dominant Union Party, the second factor leading to the failure of the constitution, was the result of a provision in it that allowed for the election of state officials on the same ballot as approval of the constitution; that is, a vote for the constitution was not only a vote for that document but also for a particular slate of officers, one chosen by William M. Stewart and his supporters. As a result, this created a large pool of individuals who were not included on the ballot but wished to be, including Stewart's convention adversary, John North, who had lost the Union Party's nomination for governor at the party convention. These disappointed office seekers, "and their names were legion, became hostile to [the constitution's] adoption."[30]

Although the constitution might have survived the mining tax issue, the split in the Union Party proved fatal to its adoption. Stewart, though unhappy with the mine provision, lobbied for passage, at least in part because he had been able to control the Union Party's nominating convention and because he assumed that "the First State Legislature would amend the new Constitution to provide taxation only of the net proceeds of productive mines,"[31] a belief based on his faith in his hand-picked slate of Union Party office seekers who supported mining interests. Indeed, Stewart was so successful at packing the official slate of candidates that David A. Johnson suggests that much of the opposition to statehood was, in fact, "based upon a widespread conviction that Stewart intended to control the new state government as a means to further his own interests and those of the mining corporation officials he represented."[32]

In the January 1864 election, the voters defeated the constitution by a vote of 8,851 to 2,157.[33] In a letter to Secretary of State William Seward later that year, Governor Nye indicated that the combination of anti-Unionists and miners had not been enough to doom the constitution, but the "dissatisfaction with some of the State ticket, and the proceedings of some of the county conventions caused its opponents to act in concert, and all combined they were strong enough to defeat it."[34] John A. Collins, a delegate to the 1864 convention, shared this belief, laying the blame for the constitution's defeat on "efforts to introduce a certain set of delegates into the State Convention.''[35] Charles E. DeLong, also a delegate to that convention, disagreed, colorfully noting that the mining tax provision had ''so stunk in the nostrils of the people'' that they rejected the 1863 constitution in its entirety.[36]

The defeat of the 1863 constitution did not, however, end the movement for statehood in Nevada Territory. In addition to the statehood desires of territory residents (shown by the overwhelming four-to-one vote in favor of statehood in the 1863 election), historian Russell Elliott suggests that at least three national circumstances led to eventual statehood for Nevada: Lincoln's need for additional votes to pass the Thirteenth Amendment abolishing slavery and ''constitution-alizing'' the Emancipation Proclamation, desires by Radical Republicans in Congress to ''secure additional votes to help ward off presidential reconstruction,'' and the need for additional Republican votes in Congress should the 1864 election be thrown into the House of Representatives.[37]

Within twenty days after voters defeated the 1863 constitution, national political pressures brought about the introduction of the Nevada Enabling Act in the Senate by Senator James R. Doolittle (R-Wisconsin) allowing the citizens of Nevada to form a state government. The bill passed both houses easily and was signed by President Lincoln on March 21, 1864. In response, Governor Nye called for new elections on June 6 to choose thirty-nine delegates for a constitutional convention, to convene on July 4. Unlike the previous four attempts at constitution writing, the 1864 effort was both authorized by Congress and, ultimately, successful.

The Constitutional Convention of 1864

The Nevada Enabling Act established a number of limitations on the convention delegates to which they faithfully adhered. Those restrictions included the following:

(1) The new State Constitution must be republican in nature and not repugnant to the Federal Constitution or the Declaration of Independence; (2) there shall be no slavery or involuntary servitude other than for punishment of crimes, without the consent of the United States and the people of Nevada; (3) the Constitutional Convention must disclaim all rights to unappropriated lands in Nevada; (4) land owned by U.S. citizens outside Nevada must not be discriminated against in taxation; and (5) there must be no taxation of federal property in the state.[38]

The congressionally authorized 1864 constitutional convention met in Carson City from July 4 through July 27. The delegates were very much like those at the 1863 convention: ten had served in the previous convention, most were from California, all but one was a member of the Union Party, and lawyers and mining interests dominated. Unlike the 1863 convention, however, antagonists John North and William M. Stewart were not delegates.[39]

Although a few delegates opposed statehood on the grounds of increased costs, a sentiment common to the antistatehood movements of the latter nineteenth century,[40] the convention as a whole supported the move toward state status, and, once again, the thirty-five delegates who came chose to name the new state "Nevada," in part because the congressional enabling act had used that name. In most other respects as well, the 1864 constitution was modeled on the failed 1863 document. Although some delegates argued for a new start based on the California Constitution, it was eventually agreed that the 1863 constitution "owed much of its substance to the California Constitution, [so] there was no point in starting all over again."[41] Furthermore, several hundred copies of the 1863 constitution were in print, saving the convention considerable time and expense.

Guttman and cluster bloc analysis of twenty-eight issues voted upon in the convention have shown that delegates, unsurprisingly, tended to divide along "economic and geographical lines," particularly in regard to divisions between mining and agricultural/ranching interests. Party affiliation was "largely meaningless . . . because all members were 'unionists.' "[42]

The 1864 constitution differed from the failed 1863 effort in two major respects, both of which had contributed to the earlier defeat. First, on the issue of taxation of mines, the convention adopted a proposal to tax only the proceeds of the mines, thus remedying the previous convention's "political indiscretion" on the issue.[43] The agricultural and ranching interests from the nonmining "cow counties" who favored retaining the 1863 language taxing mines the same as other property did so, at least in part, in the interests of equity and their resentment at having been colonized by the wealthy mining corporations in California. Cow county delegate George A. Nourse suggested that if mines were to be taxed only on their proceeds, then the constitution should also provide that "farms, and saw-mills, and other property shall be taxed only on their net proceeds"; only then would there be "some degree of fairness."[44] As to the latter, delegate A. J. Lockwood noted, "I am in favor of taxing the mines, because I want to make those gentlemen who are rolling in wealth in San Francisco, pay something for the support of our government, for the support of our common schools, and for the support of our courts."[45]

Anger and resentment over the control of Nevada's mines by rich California interests had festered for some time. In 1862, the Virginia City *Territorial Enterprise* had editorialized that "the interests of no parent country and colony could possibly be more closely united than are those of California and Nevada. The colony has untold wealth of gold and silver, and the mother country manages . . . to get it all as fast as it is dug out."[46]

Those opposed to the taxation of mines noted, however, that if the convention imposed a tax on mines equal to that of other property, it would "encumber the mining interest, which shall destroy it, or thwart its development, and you thereby strike a ruinous blow" to the state's other economic interests.[47] Delegate Charles E. DeLong warned, "But for the mines, all your stores would be removed, your farms would dry up, and be abandoned, and your wagons would stop in the streets or be turned elsewhere.''[48] And William Stewart, who had stated his opposition to the mining tax provision at the 1863 convention, held that a tax on unproductive mines would levy taxes on a ''party [who] has no property and never did have.''[49]

The debate over the mine tax issue was long and arduous, with several proposals offered by delegates on both sides. In order to prevent the total collapse of the convention, the delegates eventually compromised and adopted, by a margin of twenty-three to ten, language stating that ''[t]he legislature shall provide by law for a uniform and equal rate of assessment and taxation, . . . excepting mines and mining claims, the proceeds of which alone shall be taxed.''[50]

The compromise language left to the legislature the decision whether the ''proceeds'' would be net or gross. The leader of the moderate miners, John A. Collins, believed that ''under the circumstances it is the best thing . . . that can be done, and . . . I am compelled to vote'' for it.[51] The convention's support for the differential taxation scheme and the shift in support by six of the eight 1863 delegates who had previously voted against the plan but supported it in 1864 has been explained as a result also of the mining depression of 1864 that hit the Nevada Territory so hard that ''concern over economic survival supplanted Nevadans' fear of domination by outside interests.''[52] Nonetheless, that ''odious and unjust discrimination between different kinds of property'' led George A. Nourse to vote, along with Israel Crawford, against the constitution at the conclusion of the convention.[53]

The second major difference between the 1863 and 1864 constitutions was in the election of the state's first officials. Noting the failure of the first constitution to receive ratification by the voters, the 1864 convention did not include a slate of officers in the balloting for this constitution. The ballot on the constitution was to take place on September 7 and the election of officers on November 8, thus freeing the document of its previously fatal baggage.

The 1864 constitution was overwhelmingly supported by both the convention and the voters, just as statehood itself had been overwhelmingly supported in the 1863 election. The final day of the convention found the document supported by a vote of nineteen to two. In the September election, it was supported by a popular vote of 10,375 to 1,284.[54]

In its haste to admit Nevada as a state, the U.S. Congress had provided in the enabling act that Nevada would become a state upon the acceptance of its constitution by President Lincoln; in other words, Congress waived its right to examine and debate the constitution prior to its formal acceptance by the federal government. On October 17, the territorial government, hurrying to beat the upcoming November presidential election, wired the entire text of the state constitution to Lincoln at a cost of $3,416.77,[55] making it ''the longest and most expensive telegram ever dispatched in the United States up to that time.''[56] On October 31, 1864, President Lincoln issued the proclamation making Nevada the thirty-sixth state in the Union.

The turnaround in support for the state constitution by Nevada's voters is clearly related to the 1864 convention's decisions to tax only the proceeds of mines and to separate the vote for state officers from that of the document itself. Additionally, the mining depression of 1864 had led to strong statehood sentiment such as that expressed by the *Territorial Enterprise* newspaper: "The only hope we have of effecting a speedy and absolute cure of our crushing ills is in the adoption of a state government. . . . Better to pay even double taxes, if by doing so we can make our property ten times more productively valuable, than to pay even less and let property continue to depreciate."[57]

Even so, a good part of the support for statehood and a state constitution was based on the disreputable state of the territorial judiciary. Delegate Charles E. DeLong predicted at the 1864 convention that "many are going to vote for the Constitution in order that we may be released from the present judiciary system."[58] Thus, just as the 1858 constitution had been supported in order to rid the region of its Mormon-dominated judiciary, the 1864 constitution was supported in order to rid the area of its territorial judges.

The Nevada Territory, and before that the western Utah Territory from which it was fashioned, was a lawless region. In many respects, murders, robberies, prostitution, and gambling were the least of the judiciary's problems. More significant for the reputation of the judiciary was the clash arising from the innumerable mining suits laying claim to the prosperous Comstock Lode. As historian Hubert Howe Bancroft has observed:

Probably the first federal judges would have been able to hold their own against the criminal element in Nevada; but opposed to the combined capital and legal talent of California and Nevada, as they sometimes were, in important mining suits, they were powerless. Statutes regarding the points at issue did not exist, and the questions involved were largely determined by the rules and regulations of mining districts, and the application of common law. Immense fees were paid to able and oftentimes unprincipled lawyers, and money lavished on suborned witnesses.[59]

The most notable instance of this problem can be seen in the expensive and lengthy litigation beginning in 1861 between the Chollar and Potosi mining companies, which laid claim to the same ore deposits. Territorial district and supreme court judge G. N. Mott, who was believed to favor the Chollar Mining Company, was originally assigned the case but was either "worried or bribed into resigning" so that John W. North, who was believed to favor the Potosi Mining Company, could be appointed in his stead. A newspaper of the day charged that Mott had received $25,000 from the Potosi Company to resign.[60]

When North decided in favor of the Potosi Company in 1863, he was attacked verbally by the Chollar Company and its lawyers, including William M. Stewart, who at that time was earning an astonishing $200,000 per year to represent the interests of various mining companies. At a time when "cases were to be won through the bribing and browbeating of witnesses, juries, and justices," it has been observed that "Stewart had no equal on the [Comstock] lode."[61] The Chollar Company appealed to the territorial supreme court, where it was believed that territorial district judge and supreme court Chief Justice G. Turner favored their claim. They attempted to gain support at two dinner parties from the third justice, P. B. Locke, who was being wined and dined by the Potosi Company too.

In May 1864 Locke and North handed down the decision favoring the Potosi Company; however, Locke, whom Stewart once referred to as "the most ignorant man who ever acted in any judicial capacity in any part of the world,"[62] eventually was induced by the Chollar Company to add an addendum to his decision reopening the hearing of evidence. Again besieged by the Potosi Company, he "ordered the addendum struck off the file." Not unexpectedly, both sides were angry with Locke's unprofessional behavior. That, combined with the powerful opposition of Stewart to Judge North, led to the resignation on August 22 of North and, after a "private conference" with Stewart, Chief Justice Turner as well. Later that same day, the members of the bar convinced Judge Locke, at a final dinner party organized by Stewart, to resign also. Thus, from August 22, 1864, until the state's first officials took office in December, Nevada Territory was once again in the position of having no judiciary.[63]

The sad state of the Nevada territorial judiciary surely led many to support the 1864 constitution. Nevada's first attorney general, George A. Nourse, later observed, "Nevada became a state to escape the dead-fall of her Territorial courts. Her Temple of Justice had been transformed into a den of iniquity."[64] Although the actions of the three justices, especially Locke, "were highly irregular," there is no proof that they were actually corrupt. Indeed, Judge North eventually filed a slander suit against his old nemesis William Stewart, which he won and in which the report of the three arbitrators stated that he was "free from each and every imputation cast upon [his character] by the accusations of the defendant, William M. Stewart."[65] North, however, was not without blame; the report castigated him for having "accepted loans from 'seemingly improper' persons while judge."[66] Coming as it did in fall 1865, however, that report had little effect on the electorate's widespread perception of judicial corruption and incompetence.

The convention's distrust and lack of respect for the judiciary is evident in its adoption of a broad provision that allows judges to be removed not only by impeachment but also "for any reasonable cause . . . which may, or may not be sufficient grounds for impeachment, . . . on the vote of two-thirds of the members elected to each branch of the Legislature."[67] Thus, mining lawyers like William Stewart had at their disposal the available tools to "eliminate unfavorable judicial opinion."[68]

The effects of the convention's pragmatic decisions on mining taxes and election of state officials, the mining depression, and the state of the judiciary led to a quite different result for the 1864 constitution than its 1863 precursor. Not only was the 1864 convention and constitution different from its four predecessors in that it was duly authorized by a Congress seeking additional Republican votes; it also led to Nevada's eventual statehood after only three years as a territory.

In the November 1864 elections, the Republicans won the presidential ballot, all executive and judicial seats, and all but two of the legislative seats, affirming the Radical Republicans' hope for a new state firmly in the Republican fold. Republican H. G. Worthington was elected to the House of Representatives, and, when the legislature met in December, Republicans William Stewart and James Nye were selected the state's first U.S. senators.

NEVADA'S CONSTITUTION

During the height of the free silver battles of the 1890s, eastern politicians and press attempted to strip Nevada of its statehood,[69] but the state weathered the storm. Nevada continues to adhere to its 1864 constitution, the original document having been amended approximately 110 times. It is one of only nineteen states to function under its original constitution, an interesting comparison to, for example, Louisiana, which has operated under eleven different constitutions, and Alabama, whose constitution contains 129,000 words (Nevada's is quite short by comparison, containing only 17,000).[70]

The incredibly short span of three years from territory to statehood and the events predating and surrounding that transition make the Nevada Constitution a truly exceptional document. However, because it borrowed much from the California and the New York State constitutions, the contents of the document are not, for the most part, exceptional. Nevertheless, the document both reflects and shapes the desires of the state's citizens.

The Nevada Constitution contains nineteen articles that perform the three basic functions of all constitutions: creation of an organized government, distribution of power among the various divisions of that government, and inclusion of a bill of rights that protects individual rights from state infringement. Whereas protection of individual rights was excluded from the U.S. Constitution and only added later, the distrust of government power by the rugged individualists of the Nevada frontier—doubts sowed by the chaotic events of 1848 to 1864—is evident in the fact that the first article to the state constitution is the Declaration of Rights.

In most respects, the Nevada Constitution resembles the constitutions of the other forty-nine states more than it does the U.S. Constitution. Unlike the federal constitution but like other state constitutions, it tends to be more specific regarding limitations on the powers of the state. It is an excellent example of what Daniel J. Elazar refers to as the "Frame of Government" type of constitution. That pattern of state constitution, "found exclusively among the less populated states of the Far West," is characterized as a "business-like" document of moderate length that reflects the "relative homogeneity of the states themselves."[71] Nevada's constitution provides in a straightforward manner for a separation of powers into three branches with an extensive system of checks and balances. In addition, it creates processes for constitutional amendment and revision and vests judicial power, including judicial review, in a system of state courts. Similar to other state constitutions (except Nebraska's) it establishes a bicameral legislature and, like the other constitutions of its time and region, provides for a plural executive. During the Progressive era the document was amended to include the three forms of direct democracy popular at the time: initiative, referendum, and recall.

Constitutional Development since 1864

Given the conservative nature of Nevada's judiciary, constitutional development in the state has generally proceeded through amendment rather than by judicial activism from the bench. Under the original document, amendment could come about only through the lengthy and difficult process of gaining approval from two consecutive sessions of the state's biennial legislature and then by the voters. The addition of the initiative process in 1912 provided for a second, although equally awkward, process for amendment, which could be initiated by the citizens rather than the legislature.

Most of the over one hundred amendments to the constitution have been technical and minor in nature; however, in five areas substantive changes have been made to the original document: term of the governor, apportionment, judicial selection and discipline, suffrage and elections, and direct democracy processes. The addition of direct democracy procedures has been discussed. The other four bear brief mention here and will be examined in more detail in Part II.

Term of the Governor

The constitution of 1864 established no limit on the number of terms a governor could serve. In practice, however, no governor ever served more than two terms, and all three who attempted election to a third term failed in their reelection bids. The two-term tradition and a general distrust of government led in 1970 to passage of a two-term limitation on governors similar to that on presidents in the U.S. Constitution's Twenty-second Amendment. Like the latter, Nevada's restriction applies only to the chief executive, not to the legislature or other members of the plural executive. The legacy of this amendment has been its inherent shift in the governmental balance of power originally provided for by the convention delegates of 1864 by ensuring that all second-term governors would be lame ducks.

Apportionment

Between 1915 and 1965, the Nevada legislature was in violation of the state constitution's requirement in Article 1, section 13 that "[r]epresentation shall be apportioned according to population" and Article 15, section 13, which mandated "enumerations . . . as the basis of representation in both houses of the Legislature." In 1915 the state began, by legislative act, to apportion seats in the state senate on the basis of one per county, a so-called little federal plan similar to that in the U.S. Congress. It was not until 1950, however, that the voters approved a constitutional amendment changing Article 4, section 5 of the constitution, but not Articles 1 and 15 in a questionable attempt to legitimize this arrangement.

By the early 1960s the result, as in most other states, was gross malapportionment and underrepresentation of the state's urban areas. In 1963, for example, Clark County (Las Vegas), with 53 percent of the state's population, had only one seat in the seventeen-seat senate (5.9%) and twelve seats in the thirty-seven-seat assembly (32%).[72] After the 1964 U.S. Supreme Court decision that "little federal" plans were unconstitutional (*Reynolds v. Sims*), suit was filed in Nevada to force reapportionment of both houses, and a three-judge panel ordered the governor to call a special session of the legislature for purposes of reapportionment (*Dungan v. Sawyer*).

The cow-county-dominated legislature grudgingly did so in 1966. In 1970 the state constitution was amended once more to reestablish its original intent—and the U.S. Supreme Court's mandate—that both houses of the state legislature be apportioned according to population. The most important and obvious result of reapportionment in the state has been the shift of legislative power from the rural counties to highly urbanized Clark County, which holds a majority of seats in both houses. The substantive direction in which that shift has taken the state is difficult to measure; however, in the critical area of state funding, the shift in power to Las Vegas has resulted in increased attention to the needs of Clark County residents for educational, transportation, and other services, needs that were not particularly important to earlier rural-dominated state legislatures.

Judicial Selection and Discipline

Given Nevada's unfortunate history with its appointed territorial judges, it is no surprise that the state's constitution provides for election of the judiciary. The 1864 constitution provides for vacancies on the elective bench to be filled by gubernatorial appointment. In 1976, however, the state's voters approved an amendment establishing the Commission on Judicial Selection to present the governor with a list of three names from which he (or she) must choose one to fill the vacancy. That change effectively curbs the governor's power over judicial appointments by limiting discretion to choose.

Also added to the constitution in 1976 was a provision creating the Nevada Commission on Judicial Discipline. Made up of lawyers, judges, and laypeople, the commission has the authority to investigate the fitness of judges and censure, retire, or remove them from the bench. Thus, in addition to the public methods of recall, impeachment, and legislative removal, since 1976 a judge can, before his or her term expires, be removed or disciplined by the commission "without making his failings unnecessarily public."[73]

Suffrage and Elections

As originally adopted, Article 2, section 1 of the 1864 constitution allowed only white males age twenty-one or older to vote. Ironically, although Nevada had been "battle born" in the midst of a Civil War fought over the issue of slavery, the unionists who wrote and adopted the constitution did not see fit to allow nonwhites to vote.

In this regard, Nevadans were not unlike the inhabitants of other western states who "had a paternalistic—if condescending—interest in the few blacks who migrated to their state" but who perceived Chinese immigrants "to pose a real economic threat to . . . laborers."[74] The territorial period of Nevada exhibited tremendous discrimination against nonwhites in virtually every way. In one of its first acts, the territorial legislature provided that "no black person, or mulatto, or Indian, or Chinese should be permitted to give evidence against or in favor of any white person."[75] Similarly, cohabitation with "Indians, Chinese, or negroes [sic] was made punishable" by a fine or jail term.[76]

Although both the 1863 and 1864 constitutional conventions prohibited slavery in the new state, the delegates were "unwilling to extend rights to blacks or other nonwhites."[77] After statehood, the legislature continued that pattern with only a few exceptions, such as allowing blacks, but not Indians or Chinese, to testify against a white person.[78] Further evidence of racism came in May 1876 when the citizens of Virginia City formed the Anti-Chinese Union, passing a series of resolutions stating that "the presence of the Chinese in Nevada 'was injurious to the welfare of the State and a danger to the Republic.' ''[79]

The Fifteenth Amendment to the U.S. Constitution prohibiting restrictions on the right to vote based on race was ratified in 1870, but it was ten years before the Nevada Constitution was amended to exclude the word *white* in its suffrage provisions. Perhaps to prove a point, however, in that same 1880 election, the voters disapproved further Chinese immigration by a margin of 17,259 to 183,[80] although at that time they made up a mere 8.6 percent of the state's population.[81]

In a special election in June 1971, the state's voters barely approved a referendum reducing the voting age to eighteen. The election was close, but ultimately unnecessary given the addition in that year of the Twenty-sixth Amendment to the U.S. Constitution granting to eighteen year olds the right to vote in all federal, state, and local elections, an amendment the Nevada legislature had not ratified.

Likewise, Nevada's voters tended to be below the national curve in eliminating the poll tax. A poll tax on all males "between the ages of twenty-one and sixty years, (uncivilized American Indians excepted)" was included as Article 2, section 7 in the state constitution, but in 1910 that provision was amended to "[eliminate] the connection between paying the tax and the right to vote."[82] It was not until 1966, two years after the adoption of the Twenty-fourth Amendment to the U.S. Constitution prohibiting poll taxes, that Nevada removed that provision from its constitution.

Whereas Nevada liberalized its voting restrictions in the areas of race, age, and poll taxes only in response to federal constitutional dictates, in two other areas—women's suffrage and direct election of senators—the state led the reform movement. The Nineteenth Amendment allowing women to vote was not added to the U.S. Constitution until 1920, but women in Nevada had voted since 1914, capping a crusade that had begun in 1869 with a fiery speech in the state assembly by C. J. Hillyer, a speech that although fruitless, had been "greeted with round after round of applause."[83] To a great extent, however, credit for women's suffrage in Nevada must be given to the indefatigable Anne Martin, president of the Equal Franchise Society in Nevada, and the support given to the issue by the Populists during this era.[84]

On the issue of direct election of U.S. senators, too, the state led the way for the rest of the nation. In 1903, 1905, and 1907, a decade before the adoption of the Seventeenth Amendment in 1913, the Nevada legislature had asked Congress to "initiate the procedures necessary to obtain a constitutional amendment for the direct election of senators." And in the election of 1908, the two political parties agreed to abide by a preferential vote in the U.S. Senate race. In 1909 the legislature passed the direct primary law providing that "candidates for the United States Senate were to be nominated in the same manner as candidates for state offices."[85]

CONCLUSION

An examination of the constitutional history of Nevada illustrates vividly how state constitutions can both shape and reflect the desires of a state's citizens. The constitution operates as a window on the state's political, economic, and social structures and growth. In the materials that follow in Part II, that window will be opened wider as we examine and analyze the specific provisions of the state's often-amended and still-functional 1864 document.

NOTES

1. James W. Hulse, *The Silver State: Nevada's Heritage Reinterpreted* (Reno and Las Vegas: University of Nevada Press, 1991), 74.

2. Myron Angel, ed., *History of Nevada* (Oakland: Thompson and West, 1881, reprint ed., Berkeley: Howell-North, 1958), 32.

3. Hubert Howe Bancroft, *History of Nevada, Colorado, and Wyoming, 1540–1888* (San Francisco: History Company, 1890), 74–75.

4. Russell R. Elliott with the assistance of William D. Rowley, *History of Nevada*, 2d ed., rev. (Lincoln: University of Nebraska Press, 1987), 54.

5. Angel, *History of Nevada*, 42.

6. Elliott, *History of Nevada*, 56.

7. James W. Hulse, *The Nevada Adventure: A History*, 6th ed. (Reno: University of Nevada Press, 1990), 73.

8. Angel, *History of Nevada*, 43.

9. Bancroft, *History of Nevada, Colorado, and Wyoming*, 83–84.

10. Angel, *History of Nevada*, 49–51.

11. Gordon Morris Bakken, *Rocky Mountain Constitution Making, 1850–1912* (Westport, Conn.: Greenwood Press, 1987), 9.

12. Ibid.

13. Bancroft, *History of Nevada, Colorado, and Wyoming*, 88.

14. Elliott, *History of Nevada*, 60.

15. Angel, *History of Nevada*, 66.

16. Secretary of State, *Political History of Nevada 1990* (Carson City: State Printing Office, 1991), 55.

17. Quoted in Richard G. Lillard, *Desert Challenge: An Interpretation of Nevada* (New York: Alfred A. Knopf, 1942), 224.

18. Don W. Driggs, *The Constitution of the State of Nevada: A Commentary* (Carson City: State Printing Office, 1961), 11.

19. Eleanore Bushnell and Don W. Driggs, *The Nevada Constitution: Origin and Growth*, 6th ed. (Reno: University of Nevada Press, 1984), 13.

20. Bancroft, *History of Nevada, Colorado, and Wyoming*, 159.

21. Lillard, *Desert Challenge*, 25.

22. Elliott, *History of Nevada*, 72.

23. Ibid., 77. There is some slight disagreement among scholars on these figures. Angel, *History of Nevada*, 81, also refers to a final vote of 6,660 in favor, while Bancroft, *History of Nevada, Colorado, and Wyoming*, 178, concludes that of a total vote of 8,162, only 5,150 voted in favor of the measure. In any case, support for writing a constitution was overwhelming.

24. Secretary of State, *Political History*, 83. Elliott, *History of Nevada*, 78, claims that thirty-five of the delegates came directly from California.

25. Elliott, *History of Nevada*, 78.

26. William C. Miller and Eleanore Bushnell, eds., *Reports of the 1863 Constitutional Convention of the Territory of Nevada* (Carson City: Legislative Counsel Bureau, 1972), 273.

27. Ibid., 242.

28. Ibid., 245.

29. Ibid., 429.

30. Angel, *History of Nevada*, 84.

31. Secretary of State, *Political History*, 84.

32. David A. Johnson, "A Case of Mistaken Identity: William M. Stewart and the Rejection of Nevada's First Constitution," *Nevada Historical Quarterly 22* (Fall 1979), 188.

33. Angel, *History of Nevada*, 85.

34. Bushnell and Driggs, *Nevada Constitution*, 18.

35. Andrew J. Marsh, Official Reporter, *Official Report of the Debates and Proceedings in the Constitutional Convention of the State of Nevada* (San Francisco: Frank Eastman, 1866), 325.

36. Ibid., 224.

37. Elliott, *History of Nevada*, 83–84.

38. Secretary of State, *Political History*, 86.

39. Elliott, *History of Nevada*, 85.

40. Bakken, *Rocky Mountain Constitution Making*, 6.

41. Bushnell and Driggs, *Nevada Constitution*, 27.

42. Bakken, *Rocky Mountain Constitution Making*, 20.

43. Ibid., 52.

44. Marsh, *Debates and Proceedings*, 224.

45. Ibid., 356.

46. Quoted in Lillard, *Desert Challenge*, 75.

47. Marsh, *Debates and Proceedings*, 361.

48. Ibid., 335.

49. Miller and Bushnell, *Reports*, 242.

50. Marsh, *Debates and Proceedings*, 444, 446.

51. Ibid., 444.

52. Johnson, "A Case of Mistaken Identity," 198.

53. Marsh, *Debates and Proceedings*, 820, 827.

54. Ibid., xiv, 827. Gilman M. Ostrander, *Nevada: The Great Rotten Borough, 1859–1964* (New York: Alfred A. Knopf, 1966), 39, puts the tally at 6,530 to 2,260.

55. Effie Mona Mack, Idel Anderson, and Beulah E. Singleton, *Nevada Government: A Study of the Administration and Politics of State, County, Township, and Cities* (Caldwell, Idaho: Caxton Printers, Ltd., 1953), 15.

56. Secretary of State, *Political History*, 90.

57. *Virginia City Territorial Enterprise*, August 19, 1864, quoted in Bushnell and Driggs, *Nevada Constitution*, 42.

58. Marsh, *Debates and Proceedings*, 173.

59. Bancroft, *History of Nevada, Colorado, and Wyoming*, 172.

60. *Virginia City Territorial Enterprise*, quoted in Samuel P. Davis, ed., *The History of Nevada*, 2 vols. (Reno: Elms Publishing Co., 1913), 288.

61. Ostrander, *Great Rotten Borough*, 28.

62. William M. Stewart, *Reminiscences of Senator William M. Stewart of Nevada*, ed. George Rothwell Brown (New York: Neal Publishing Co., 1908), 153.

63. This entire episode can be found in Bancroft, *History of Nevada, Colorado, and Wyoming*, 173–75. According to Stewart's memoirs, Turner had accepted a $5,000 bribe for issuing an injunction in an important mining case. In their "private conference," Stewart threatened to swear out a court warrant for Turner's arrest on bribery charges if he did not resign. William M. Stewart, *Reminiscences*, 160–61.

64. Davis, *History of Nevada*, 302.

65. *Washoe Times*, September 21, 1863, quoted in Elliott, *History of Nevada*, 87.

66. Ostrander, *Great Rotten Borough*, 32–33. In his biography of William M. Stewart, Russell Elliott notes that North had accepted a loan from the Potosi Mine owners in order to build a mill in Washoe City knowing that "he might have to adjudicate the [Potosi-Chollar] issue." Russell Elliott, *Servant of Power: A Political Biography of Senator William M. Stewart* (Reno: University of Nevada Press, 1983), 22.

67. Marsh, *Debates and Proceedings*, 844.

68. Bakken, *Rocky Mountain Constitution Making*, 40.

69. Mary Ellen Glass, *Silver and Politics in Nevada: 1892–1902* (Reno: University of Nevada Press, 1969), 76.

70. Bushnell and Driggs, *Nevada Constitution*, 43.

71. Daniel J. Elazar, "The Principles and Traditions Underlying State Constitutions," *Publius: The Journal of Federalism* 12 (Winter 1982), 21–22.

72. Hulse, *Nevada Adventure*, 258.

73. Bushnell and Driggs, *Nevada Constitution*, 139.

74. James Edward Wright, *The Politics of Populism: Dissent in Colorado* (New Haven: Yale University Press, 1974), 26.

75. Bancroft, *History of Nevada, Colorado, and Wyoming*, 160.

76. Ibid., 162.

77. Elmer R. Rusco, *"Good Time Coming?" Black Nevadans in the Nineteenth Century* (Westport, Conn.: Greenwood Press, 1975), 29.

78. Ibid., 37.

79. Russell M. Magnaghi, "Virginia City's Chinese Community, 1860–1880," *Nevada Historical Society Quarterly* 24 (Summer 1981), 153.

80. Bancroft, *History of Nevada, Colorado, and Wyoming*, 204.

81. Sue Fawn Chung, "The Chinese Experience in Nevada: Success Despite Discrimination," *Nevada Public Affairs Review*, no. 2 (1987), 44.

82. Bushnell and Driggs, *Nevada Constitution*, 40.

83. Hulse, *Silver State*, 159.

84. Robert W. Larson, *Populism in the Mountain West* (Albuquerque: University of New Mexico Press, 1986), 155.

85. Elliott, *History of Nevada*, 244–45.

Part II

Nevada Constitution and Commentary

Part II provides a section-by-section analysis of the Nevada Constitution. Each section examines the origins of the provision and its interpretation by the courts and, where applicable, the attorney general. Citations to cases appear in the Table of Cases at the end of the book.

The analysis provided here does not purport to be comprehensive or exhaustive. It covers many of the major interpretive issues that have arisen over the years, but it does not include all of them or those that may arise in the future. Readers should not rely upon this work for legal advice and are cautioned to consult an attorney regarding specific legal questions.

The spelling and capitalization used in the text below have been retained from the original document. The leadlines have been added by the Legislative Counsel Bureau of the State of Nevada.

PRELIMINARY ACTION

WHEREAS, The Act of Congress Approved March Twenty First A.D. Eighteen Hundred and Sixty Four "To enable the People of the Territory of Nevada to form a Constitution and State Government and for the admission of such State into the Union on an equal footing with the Original States," requires that the Members of the Convention for framing said Constitution shall, after Organization, on behalf of the people of said Territory, adopt the Constitution of the United States.—Therefore, Be it Resolved,

That the Members of this Convention elected by the Authority of the aforesaid enabling Act of Congress, Assembled in Carson City, the Capital of said Territory of Nevada, and immediately subsequent to its Organization,

do adopt, on behalf of the people of said Territory the Constitution of the
United States.

ORDINANCE

Slavery prohibited; freedom of religious worship; disclaimer of public lands

In obedience to the requirements of an act of the Congress of the United
States, approved March twenty-first, A.D. eighteen hundred and sixty-four,
to enable the people of Nevada to form a constitution and state government,
this convention, elected and convened in obedience to said enabling act, do
ordain as follows, and this ordinance shall be irrevocable, without the consent
of the United States and the people of the State of Nevada.

First. That there shall be in this state neither slavery nor involuntary
servitude, otherwise than in the punishment for crimes, whereof the party
shall have been duly convicted.

Second. That perfect toleration of religious sentiment shall be secured,
and no inhabitant of said state shall ever be molested, in person or property,
on account of his or her mode of religious worship.

Third. That the people inhabiting this territory do agree and declare, that
they forever disclaim all right and title to the unappropriated public lands
lying within said territory, and that the same shall be and remain at the sole
and entire disposition of the United States; and that lands belonging to citizens
of the United States, residing without the said state, shall never be taxed
higher than the land belonging to the residents thereof; and that no taxes
shall be imposed by said state on lands or property therein belonging to, or
which may hereafter be purchased by, the United States, unless otherwise
provided by the congress of the United States.

Congress had established five limitations on the convention delegates in the 1864
Nevada Enabling Act. The resolutions entitled "Preliminary Action" and "Ordinance" adopt those constraints. The Preliminary Action adopts the U.S. Constitution as the supreme law of the land, and the Ordinance adopts the prohibition
on slavery, affirmatively states official toleration of religious sentiment, disclaims
all unappropriated land in the territory, and prohibits a higher rate of taxation
than on residents for nonresident landowners who are U.S. citizens. Unlike other
provisions of the constitution, which are revocable, the Ordinance specifically
states that it cannot be revoked without the approval of both the U.S. government
and the people of the state.

To date, the irrevocability provision has not been tested in the courts and it
is unclear whether the state does, in fact, retain its sovereign power on an "equal
footing" with other states to revoke this Ordinance.[1] It has, however, been
amended on one occasion. In 1956, the phrase, "unless otherwise provided by

the Congress of the United States,'' was added in order to allow the state to take advantage of any changes by Congress that might allow the taxation of federal property. Given that 87 percent of the land in Nevada is owned by the federal government, that change would provide a windfall in revenue to the state's coffers.

PREAMBLE

> We the people of the State of Nevada Grateful to Almighty God for our freedom in order to secure its blessings, insure domestic tranquility, and form a more perfect Government, do establish this CONSTITUTION.

Like the Preamble to the U.S. Constitution, the Nevada Constitution's Preamble serves merely as a prologue; it does not grant or limit any powers of the state government. Unlike the federal constitution, however, it expresses gratitude to God for the opportunity to create a ''more perfect Government,'' presumably one ''more perfect'' than the controversial territorial government to which statehood was a reaction. Given the chronic lawlessness existing in Nevada during the territorial period, it is, perhaps, not surprising that a major philosophical underpinning and purpose of the state's constitution was to ''insure domestic tranquility.''

Article 1

Declaration of Rights

At the time of the adoption of the Nevada Constitution in 1864, the federal Bill of Rights had been held not applicable to the states. In the 1833 case of *Barron v. Baltimore*, the U.S. Supreme Court held that the limitations included within the first ten amendments restricted only the federal government, not the states. Consequently, states were free to infringe upon speech and press and could deny due process to criminal defendants without violating the U.S. Constitution.

The only restrictions that were applicable to the states were a few civil liberties protections included within the original Constitution (e.g., no ex post facto laws) and whatever restrictions a state may have had in its own state constitution. Consequently, the delegates to Nevada's 1864 convention included within Article 1 civil liberties protections that were to be outside the authority of the state government to infringe.

With passage of the Fourteenth Amendment in 1868, the due process clause was opened as an avenue for the U.S. Supreme Court eventually to apply most of the provisions of the Bill of Rights to the states. Through the process of "incorporation," all but five of the twenty-two protections of the Constitution's first eight amendments are now applicable to the states.[2]

The process of incorporation does not render state bills of rights obsolete. Some state judiciaries have interpreted their state bills of rights as providing greater civil liberties protections to their citizens than does the federal bill of rights (e.g., California, New York, and New Jersey).[3] Nevada has not done so, and the pattern has been to interpret state constitutional guarantees parallel to similar clauses in the federal Bill of Rights.

Sec: 1. **Inalienable Rights**

> All men are by Nature free and equal and have certain inalienable rights among which are those of enjoying and defending life and liberty; Acquiring, Possessing and Protecting property and pursuing and obtaining safety and happiness.

This section is taken from the Declaration of Independence, which was derivative of John Locke's social contract theories. Locke had argued that the purpose of government was to protect the natural rights of life, liberty, and property.

The provisions of this section have been read to guarantee a "right to freedom and equality" (*Atteberry v. State*); however, the state may pass regulations infringing upon that freedom as an exercise of its police power to protect the health, safety, welfare, and morals of its citizens (Attorney General's Opinion 82–15, June 25, 1982). The state, for example, may give preference to veterans in public employment (Attorney General's Opinion 167, May 27, 1935) and prohibit the possession of weapons without a permit (Attorney General's Opinion 82–15, June 25, 1982). However, the right to protect one's life and property in the courts includes the protection from unreasonable and discriminatory court fees (Attorney General's Opinion 425, February 28, 1947).

Sec: 2. **Purpose of government; paramount allegiance to United States**

> All political power is inherent in the people. Government is instituted for the protection, security and benefit of the people; and they have the right to alter or reform the same whenever the public good may require it. But the Paramount Allegiance of every citizen is due to the Federal Government in the exercise of all its Constitutional powers as the same have been or may be defined by the Supreme Court of the United States; and no power exists in the people of this or any other State of the Federal Union to dissolve their connection therewith or perform any act tending to impair, subvert, or resist the Supreme Authority of the government of the United States. The Constitution of the United States confers full power on the Federal Government to maintain and Perpetuate its existance [*sic*], and whensoever any portion of the States, or people thereof attempt to secede from the Federal Union, or may forcibly resist the Execution of its laws, the Federal Government may, by warrant of the Constitution, employ armed force in compelling obedience to its Authority.

It is not surprising, given the fact that Nevada became a state in the midst of the Civil War, that this firm pledge of allegiance to the federal government and rejection of secession was included in the constitution. The major debate at the convention was whether this provision should refer to the decisions of all federal courts or only the U.S. Supreme Court. The delegates opted for the latter, a decision interpreted to mean that although the state supreme court is "bound by the decisions of the United States Supreme Court, it is not bound by the decisions of the other federal courts" (*Bargas v. Warden, Nevada State Prison*).

Sec: 3. Trial by jury; waiver in civil cases

> The right of trial by Jury shall be secured to all and remain inviolate forever; but a Jury trial may be waived by the parties in all civil cases in the manner to be prescribed by law; and in civil cases, if three fourths of the Jurors agree upon a verdict it shall stand and have the same force and effect as a verdict by the whole Jury, Provided, the Legislature by a law passed by a two thirds vote of all the members elected to each branch thereof may require a unanimous verdict notwithstanding this Provision.

The right to a jury trial exists not only for the protection of the accused but also for the protection of "the whole people" (*State v. McClear; Rains v. State*) to ensure that justice is done and a fair decision results.

This section differs somewhat from the U.S. Constitution's Seventh Amendment, which specifically requires jury trials in federal civil cases when over twenty dollars is at stake. Whatever common law rights to civil trials existed at the time of the adoption of the state constitution are protected by this provision (*State ex rel. Fletcher v. Ruhe*); it does not, however, confer any additional rights that did not exist at the time (*Hudson v. City of Las Vegas; Close v. Isbell Construction Company*). A jury trial is required, however, in "serious" cases (e.g., simple assault or battery) even though they might not have been afforded at common law (Attorney General's Opinion 85–16, October 2, 1985).

In criminal cases, the right to a jury trial depends on whether the offense charged is "serious" or "petty," a determination made by examining the "maximum authorized penalty" for the offense (*State v. Smith*, 1983). The right to a jury trial in criminal cases in Nevada has been determined to be "coextensive with that guaranteed by the [Sixth Amendment to] the federal constitution" (*Blanton v. North Las Vegas*). The U.S. Supreme Court has held that "petty" offenses are those punishable by no more than six months in prison and a five hundred dollar fine (*Dyke v. Taylor Implement Manufacturing Company*).

Although criminal juries in Nevada must reach a unanimous verdict, only three-fourths of the jury is required to agree on a verdict in a civil case. Over the objections of some of the cow-county delegates at the convention, it was ultimately decided that the territorial experience with hung juries, often after bribery by one of the wealthy mining companies party to most civil litigation, required experimentation with a less-than-unanimous verdict. Apparently they believed it would be more difficult to bribe four jurors than one. However, because the three-fourths verdict had not been tried elsewhere, the delegates authorized the legislature to require unanimous verdicts in civil cases if the experiment proved to be a failure.

This right necessarily implies a right to an impartial jury, defined as one in which the jurors "are not interested in the event of the suit, and . . . have no such bias or prejudice in favor of or against either party as would render them partial toward either party" (*State v. McClear*). Although the legislature may regulate the means of determining how a juror's impartiality is ascertained, it cannot deny the basic right to an impartial jury (*State v. Ah Sam*). Defendants are guaranteed by this section the right to challenge jurors for cause or actual bias *(State v. Raymond; State v. McClear)*.

Although this section appears to restrict its waiver provisions to civil trials, the Nevada Supreme Court has held that the right to a jury trial in criminal cases may also be waived (*Rains v. State*). Any such waiver must be indicated in the record (*Murrish v. Kennedy*), and a defendant who waives a jury trial cannot later appeal on the grounds that he or she was denied a jury verdict (*Rains v. State*).

Sec: 4. **Liberty of conscience**

The free exercise and enjoyment of religious profession and worship without discrimination or preference shall forever be allowed in this State, and no person shall be rendered incompetent to be a witness on account of his opinions on matters of his religious belief, but the liberty of consciene [*sic*] hereby secured, shall not be so construed, as to excuse acts of licentiousness or justify practices inconsistent with the peace, or safety of this State.

Consistent with the terms of the congressional enabling act, this section and the Ordinance guarantee the freedom of religious worship. In addition to these two "free exercise" provisions, sections 2, 9, and 10 of Article 11 erect "no establishment" provisions prohibiting the use of public funds for sectarian instruction or purposes.

There was some debate at the convention over the necessity of including this section because it was repetitive of the Ordinance. It was included, in part, because the prohibition on licentiousness, not contained in the Ordinance, was assumed to "[shut] up the bars . . . against polygamy," as was practiced by Mormons of the time.[4]

This section prohibits the legislature "from making any law respecting establishment of religion or free exercise thereof" (Attorney General's Opinion 320, March 3, 1954). There has been no significant interpretation of this section.

Sec: 5. **Suspension of habeas corpus**

The privilege of the writ of Habeas Corpus, shall not be suspended unless when in cases of rebellion or invasion the public safety may require its suspension.

The writ of habeas corpus is a significant civil liberty designed to protect individuals from arbitrary executive action. An individual held in custody may petition a court for a writ of habeas corpus; if the executive officer holding that individual cannot justify detention, the court will issue the writ, freeing the prisoner.

The legislature has the authority to regulate the use of the writ of habeas corpus in the state but lacks power to abolish it entirely (*Grego v. Sheriff, Clark County*).

In an effort to eliminate much of the litigation resulting from the abuse of the writ of habeas corpus by jailhouse lawyers, the Nevada Supreme Court has held that a court is not required to consider successive petitions by a prisoner that "contain grounds for relief which could have been raised in prior petitions" (*Dromiack v. Warden, Nevada State Prison*). (See also the discussion under Article 6, section 6.)

Sec: 6. **Excessive bails and fines; cruel or unusual punishments; detention of witnesses**

> Excessive bail shall not be required, nor excessive fines imposed, nor shall cruel and unusual punishments be inflicted, nor shall witnesses be unreasonably detained.

Sections 6, 7, and 8 of this article contain restrictions on courts in their exercise of the judicial power conferred upon them by Article 6. What is "excessive" or "cruel" or "unreasonable" is, of course, subject to much debate and interpretation. A punishment may be cruel and unusual if it is "so disproportionate to the crime for which it is inflicted that it shocks the conscience and offends fundamental notions of human dignity" (*Schmidt v. State*). Thus, a statute authorizing a vasectomy for individuals convicted of rape was unconstitutional (*Mickle v. Henrichs*), whereas a sentence of six years for repeated incidents of indecent exposure was not (*Schmidt v. State*).

In line with U.S. Supreme Court pronouncements in this area, the Nevada legislature has provided a two-tier proceeding in capital cases: an adjudication of guilt and a separate penalty proceeding at which mitigating and aggravating factors are assessed.

Sec: 7. **Bail; exception for capital offenses and certain murders**

> All persons shall be bailable on sufficient sureties; unless for Capital Offenses or murders punishable by life imprisonment without possibility of parole when the proof is evident or the presumption great.

The phrase "or murders punishable by life imprisonment without possibility of parole" was added by amendment in 1980. In general, the import of this section is that an individual is considered innocent until proved guilty and is entitled to bail absolutely in noncapital cases and in capital cases with some exceptions (*In re Wheeler*). Thus, even in a capital case, unless the proof is "evident" or the presumption "great," the accused is entitled to bail (*Ex parte Nagel; State v. Teeter*). After conviction, bail is entirely discretionary (*State v. McFarlin*).

Under the right to bail of this section and the restrictions in section 6, bail cannot be so excessive "as to preclude its being given" (*Ex parte Malley*).

In determining whether proof is "evident" or the presumption "great," the courts are granted broad discretion. Although it is not necessary to show proof of guilt beyond a reasonable doubt in denying bail (*In re Wheeler*), it is necessary to show more than a "mere inference of guilt" (*Howard v. Sheriff of Clark County*) or the mere existence of the "probable cause" necessary for arrest and trial (*Hanley v. State*).

Sec: 8. Rights of accused in criminal prosecutions; jeopardy; due process of law; eminent domain

> No person shall be tried for a capital or other infamous crime (except in cases of impeachment, and in cases of the militia when in actual service and the land and naval forces in time of war, or which this state may keep, with the consent of congress, in time of peace, and in cases of petit larceny, under the regulation of the legislature) except on presentment or indictment of the grand jury, or upon information duly filed by a district attorney, or attorney-general of the state, and in any trial, in any court whatever, the party accused shall be allowed to appear and defend in person, and with counsel, as in civil actions. No person shall be subject to be twice put in jeopardy for the same offense; nor shall he be compelled, in any criminal case, to be a witness against himself, nor be deprived of life, liberty, or property, without due process of law; nor shall private property be taken for public use without just compensation having been first made, or secured, except in cases of war, riot, fire, or great public peril, in which case compensation shall be afterward made.

This section, similar to the U.S. Constitution's Fifth Amendment, is an omnibus one, containing five separate protections for criminal defendants—indictment/information, defense counsel, double jeopardy, self-incrimination, and due process of law—and one for property owners—eminent domain.

Indictment or Information

The 1864 convention, "with little experience, a tendency to borrow, and no sense of urgency," chose to retain the common law grand jury system.[5] In 1912, this section was amended to allow also for prosecution of crimes by an "information" filed by a district attorney or the attorney general. Neither of these procedures "violates any fundamental concept of ordered liberty essential to a fair prosecution" (*United States ex rel. Morford v. Hocker*). Because the Fifth Amendment grand jury clause has not been applied to the states, it is the prerogative of the prosecutor, absent any statutory limitations, to proceed by grand jury indictment or information (*State v. Maes*).

The grand jury provisions of this section are not self-executing (*Ryan v. Eighth Judicial District Court ex rel. County of Clark*); it is left to the legislature to prescribe how such indictments are to be formed (*State v. Millain*).

Defense Counsel

The Sixth Amendment right to counsel was held applicable to the states in the U.S. Supreme Court's decision in *Gideon v. Wainwright*. Thus, an indigent criminal defendant is entitled to have an attorney appointed in all federal and state prosecutions for "serious" offenses, defined as those in which there is a potential loss of liberty by incarceration (*Argersinger v. Hamlin*).

The terms of this section do not prohibit an individual from self-representation in court, referred to as *pro se* representation, so long as the waiver of counsel is made "knowingly and intelligently" (*Miller v. State*). Nevertheless, the court is responsible for informing the defendant of the "danger and disadvantages of self representation [so that he will] make his choice with his eyes open" (*Hollis v. State*). Counsel may be forced upon a defendant only if, in the opinion of the court, "it appears during the course of the proceedings that counsel should be present either to advise or conduct the defense" (*Miller v. State*).

Although this section states that an individual has the right "to appear and defend in person, *and* with counsel," a defendant is required to choose one form of representation or the other. A defendant cannot have a case presented by himself and counsel or by either acting alternatively. An individual who chooses self-representation cannot interrupt the trial to demand counsel or "later complain that he was not represented by counsel" (*Miller v. State*). The court, however, must give a *pro se* defendant time to prepare a defense (*Colgain v. State*).

The right to counsel protected by this section includes not only criminal prosecutions by civil authorities but also any courts-martial prosecuted under state law (*State ex rel. Huffaker v. Crosby*).

Double Jeopardy

The prohibition of double jeopardy prevents an individual from being retried for the same offense by the same jurisdiction once he or she has been acquitted. Jeopardy attaches to a defendant once the jury has been impaneled and sworn or when the judge begins to hear the case (*State v. Blackwell; Carter v. State*).

Once jeopardy has attached, the trial must be completed absent consent of the defendant (*Wheeler v. Second Judicial District Court; Gaitor v. State; Melchor-Gloria v. State*) or "manifest necessity" such as the failure of the jury to reach a verdict (*Ex parte Maxwell*) or the unavailability of a witness for which the prosecutor is not responsible (*State v. Connery; Hylton v. Eighth Judicial District Court*).

Even in cases where jeopardy may have attached, the courts have recognized limits to the prohibition on double jeopardy. A defendant may face both criminal and civil action for a single offense (such as an accident resulting from drunken driving) since one is an offense against the criminal law and the other a reparation for damages done to an individual (*Brown v. Evans*). Similarly, a prison inmate may be tried for offenses committed while incarcerated even if previously disciplined by prison authorities for the same acts (*Shuman v. Sheriff of Carson City*). An individual may be tried for a lesser offense (e.g., battery) even though acquitted of a more serious offense (e.g., murder) when "each [offense] requires proof of a fact which the other does not" (*Meador v. State; Colley v. Sumner*).

An individual may be tried by state and federal courts for the same offense if that offense violated both state and federal law. For instance, the offense of murder may violate both state (murder) statutes and federal (civil rights) statutes, and an acquittal in one jurisdiction does not immunize a defendant from trial in the other (*United States v. Lanza*).

Self-Incrimination

The protection from self-incrimination prohibits the police and their "agents" (e.g., a convict placed in a cell in order to gain incriminating testimony from the defendant) from physically or psychologically coercing an individual to testify against himself or herself (*Holyfield v. State*). A defendant who exercises this right not to self-incriminate cannot be punished for that exercise by derogatory comments of the prosecutor or judge to the jury that the individual failed to testify in his or her own behalf (*Washington v. State*).

A grant of immunity from prosecution negates the protection from self-incrimination as the defendant is no longer in fear of prosecution. The protection does not extend to nontestimonial evidence, such as hair and writing samples, or physical characteristics, such as tattoos (*State v. Ah Chuey*).

Due Process of Law

The due process language of this section, identical to that of the Fifth and Fourteenth amendments of the U.S. Constitution, protects citizens from arbitrary, personal, or capricious action by government officials. Its purpose is to ensure fundamental fairness in government treatment of all individuals.

Although the federal courts have been required to define the substantive nature of "liberty" and "property," the Nevada courts have primarily been called upon to determine the procedural rights protected by due process. The attorney general, however, has held that the death penalty does not violate substantive due process rights (Attorney General's Opinion 11, February 2, 1971). That office has also determined that substantive due process employment rights are guaranteed under this section to work without being required to join a union (Attorney General's Opinion 407, September 22, 1958) and for a physician to maintain a license (Attorney General's Opinion 1, May 5, 1914).

A preliminary hearing prior to trial is not required by due process of law (*Seim v. State*). One has the right to be notified of pending action against oneself (*Mitchell v. Second Judicial District Court*), and at trial a defendant is entitled to "establish any fact which . . . would be a protection to himself or his property" (*Wright v. Cradlebaugh; State v. Fouquette*). A conviction based on perjured testimony is so unfair as to violate due process (*Riley v. State*).

Due process requires that an individual have fair notice or warning of what constitutes illegal conduct. A statute or ordinance that is so vague that "men of common intelligence must necessarily guess at its meaning, and differ as to its application" violates this section (*Eaves v. Board of Clark County Commissioners*).

In general, due process of law requires at a minimum that all rules enforced by government be reasonably or rationally related to a legitimate state purpose. A mandatory motorcycle helmet law, for example, is permissible because it rationally relates to the state's legitimate interest in safety (*State v. Eighth Judicial District Court ex rel. State*), but a law that prohibits delivery of gasoline to underground tanks by trucks over a particular size violates due process because it is not reasonably related to a legitimate state purpose (*In re Martin*).

Eminent Domain

This section authorizes the state to take private property for public use (Article 8, section 7 allows the taking of property for the use of corporations). It is similar to the Fifth Amendment of the U.S. Constitution in that it requires just compensation to be given to the private property owner; it differs from the federal protection in requiring that the compensation be made or tendered prior to the taking, although a property owner may waive the right to payment prior to taking (*Saunders v. State ex rel. Department of Highways*).

Although the method of taking is left to legislative discretion (*Virginia & T.R.R. v. Elliott*), the legislature lacks power to abridge or impair this right (*Alper v. Clark County*).

The Nevada courts have held that "just compensation" means "real, substantial, full and ample" compensation (*Virginia & T.R.R. v. Elliott*). Anyone who believes that property has been taken without just compensation may file suit in court for remedy. In determining what is just, the courts must see that the property is valued "in light of its highest and best use" (*Sorenson v. State ex rel. Department of Highways*) and by the value of the property to the condemnee, not the condemnor (*Stagecoach Utilities, Inc. v. Stagecoach General Import Distributors*).

Sec: 9. **Liberty of speech and the press**

> Every citizen may freely speak, write and publish his sentiment on all subjects
> being responsible for the abuse of that right; and no law shall be passed to
> restrain or abridge the liberty of speech or of the press. In all criminal
> prosecutions and civil actions for libels, the truth may be given in evidence
> to the Jury; and if it shall appear to the Jury that the matter charged as
> libelous is true and was published with good motives and for justifiable
> ends, the party shall be acquitted or exonerated.

The application of the speech and press protections of the First Amendment to
the states in the 1930s did not make this section obsolete. The state courts can,
although they have not, interpret these state provisions to grant greater protection
than the federal Bill of Rights.

In a broad interpretation of these rights, the state courts have held that expression
rights are not limited to public speeches and pamphlets but to "every form
and manner of dissemination of ideas held by the people," including peaceful
picketing (*State ex rel. Culinary Workers Union, Local 226 v. Eighth Judicial
District Court ex rel. Clark County*) and distribution of handbills (*In re Philipie*).
Statements of opinion and statements made in good faith are protected by this
section (*Reynolds v. Arentz*). However, abuse of speech rights, such as picketing
in a violent manner, is not protected from governmental limitation (*State ex rel.
Culinary Workers Union, Local 226 v. Eighth Judicial District Court ex rel.
Clark County*).

Generally the press may publish information in its possession (*Near v. Minnesota;
New York Times v. United States*). However, there has been debate over
the issue of limiting access to information to the press. The Nevada courts have
held that the press does not have a right of "access to sources for gathering
information not available to the general public . . . [and it] enjoys no greater
privilege than any other individual citizen" (*Azbill v. Fisher*). Thus, the press
can be kept from maximum security areas of prisons, the atomic testing site,
and disaster areas if the public generally is not given access to these areas.

Sec: 10. **Right to assemble and to petition**

> The people shall have the right freely to assemble together to consult for
> the common good, to instruct their representatives and to petition the Leg-
> islature for redress of Grievances.

The First Amendment right of assembly was applied to the states in the U.S.
Supreme Court's 1937 decision in *DeJonge v. Oregon*. This section has not been
subject to significant interpretation.

Sec: 11. **Right to keep and bear arms; civil power supreme**

1. Every citizen has the right to keep and bear arms for security and defense, for lawful hunting and recreational use and for other lawful purposes.

2. The military shall be subordinate to the civil power; No standing army shall be maintained by this State in time of peace, and in time of War, no appropriation for a standing army shall be for a longer time than two years.

The Second Amendment, guaranteeing the right to keep and bear arms, has not been applied to the states. Therefore, although the federal government arguably may not prohibit gun ownership, the states are free to do so absent any state statutory or constitutional prohibitions. In the face of growing support at the national level for gun control laws, this section was amended in 1982 to add paragraph 1. Neither it nor paragraph 2, establishing civilian control over the state militia, has been subject to interpretation.

Sec: 12. **Quartering soldier in private house**

No soldier shall, in time of Peace be quartered in any house without the consent of the owner, nor in time of War, except in the manner to be prescribed by law.

This section is similar to the Third Amendment of the Bill of Rights. Because that amendment has not been held applicable to the states, section 12 provides the only protection at the state level from quartering of troops in private homes. It has not been subject to interpretation.

Sec: 13. **Representation apportioned according to population**

Representation shall be apportioned according to population.

This requirement, designed to ensure that representation in the state is based on population, was "intended to secure to the citizen an equal representation in making the laws of the state" (*State ex rel. Winnie v. Stoddard*). This intent has not always been fulfilled, however. Between 1915 and 1965 the state senate was apportioned on the basis of one senator per county. In 1950 Article 4, section 5 was amended to legitimize this "little federal" plan arrangement, but neither this article nor Article 15, section 13, requiring "enumeration . . . as the basis of representation in both houses of the legislature," was changed.

The requirement of equal apportionment contained in this section applies not only to the legislature but also to other governing bodies, such as city councils (*State ex rel. Fletcher v. Ruhe*) and county commissions (*County of Clark v. City of Las Vegas*).

Although apportionment does not require mathematical exactitude, large disparities in the population of districts will not be permitted. Thus, a county commission apportionment plan in which population disparities between districts "range from −20.2% to 25.2% of the norm" was deemed offensive to the one person–one vote principle (*County of Clark v. City of Las Vegas*).

Although malapportionment is prohibited by this section, gerrymandering—the redrawing of districts in order to "enhance the political fortunes of the party in power (or incumbents), as opposed to creating a district with geographic compactness"—is not.[6] The legislature that meets in session after the decennial census is therefore in a unique position to draw district lines solidifying the hold of incumbents or a particular party on that body. Even here, however, the state legislature's power is limited by the U.S. Supreme Court's decision in *Davis v. Bandemer*, which says that political gerrymandering is a justiciable issue. Political gerrymandering is unconstitutional when there is intent to discriminate and the effect of the gerrymandering is to "consistently degrade a voter's or a group of voters' influence on the political process as a whole" for more than a decade with no hope that they will do better after the next reapportionment.

Sec: 14. **Exemption of property from execution; imprisonment for debt**

The privilege of the debtor to enjoy the necessary comforts of life shall be recognized by wholesome laws, exempting a reasonable amount of property from seizure or sale for payment of any debts or liabilities hereafter contracted; And there shall be no imprisonment for debt, except in cases of fraud, libel, or slander, and no person shall be imprisioned [*sic*] for a Militia fine in time of Peace.

This section prohibits imprisonment of debtors except in cases of fraudulent or tortious actions (*Ex parte Bergman*). Because the terms of this section do not apply to alimony or child support debts, an individual who fails to make these court-ordered payments can be jailed for contempt (*Ex parte Phillips; Lamb v. Lamb*). (See the discussion under Article 4, section 30 for the exemption of homesteads from seizure for repayment of debts.)

Sec: 15. **Bill of attainder; ex post facto law; obligation of contract**

No bill of attainder, ex-post-facto law, or law impairing the obligation of contracts shall ever be passed.

This section is probably unnecessary because Article I, section 10 of the U.S. Constitution prohibits states from passing ex post facto laws, bills of attainder, and laws impairing the obligation of contracts. Nevertheless, its presence in the state constitution suggests its importance to the 1864 convention delegates.

Bills of attainder and ex post facto laws are designed to prevent legislative abuse of power in the punishment of political enemies or disfavored classes. A bill of attainder is an act passed by the legislature that "applies to named individuals or to easily ascertainable members of a group in such way as to inflict punishment on them without a judicial trial" (*Oueilhe v. Lovell*). An ex post facto law is one that "makes criminal an act which was innocent when done; it is retrospective in its application" (*Dunphy v. Sheehan*). Civil laws that act retrospectively may violate due process in some cases but are not violations of the prohibition on ex post facto laws, which is restricted to criminal statutes (*United States v. Darusmont*). To be invalid, an ex post facto law must work to the disadvantage of the accused. A statute diminishing the penalties of a crime would not violate this section, but a law passed after the commission of an offense that "inflicts a greater punishment than the law annexed to the crime at the time it was committed" it would be invalid (*Goldsworthy v. Hannifin*).

The contract clause in this section prohibits the state from interfering in the obligation of a contract. A statute that provided for a moratorium on the foreclosure of mortgages for two years was held to violate this prohibition (Attorney General's Opinion 95, January 26, 1933), as was a law requiring a water district to supply water to certain individuals without compensation (Attorney General's Opinion 28, March 26, 1959).

The legislature is not prohibited by this section from passing laws in the exercise of its police power that benefit the public even if such laws impair previously entered contracts (*Koscot Interplanetary, Inc. v. Draney*). The general rule applicable in these situations is that a right vested by ordinance or statute may be modified or repealed only if "(1) the right to do so was reserved in the ordinance, (2) in the proper exercise of the police power, or (3) with the consent of the persons claiming the right" (Attorney General's Opinion 270, October 26, 1965).

Sec: 16. Rights of foreigners

[Repealed in 1924.]

Prior to its repeal, this section stated that "foreigners who are, or who may hereafter become Bona-fide residents of this State, shall enjoy the same rights, in respect to the possession, enjoyment and inheritance of property, as native born citizens."

Sec: 17. Slavery and involuntary servitude prohibited

Neither Slavery nor involuntary servitude unless for the punishment of crimes shall ever be tolerated in this State.

This section, which parallels that in the Ordinance, was required by the terms of the Civil War era congressional enabling act. It has not been subject to interpretation.

Sec: 18. **Unreasonable seizure and search; issuance of warrants**

> The right of the people to be secure in their persons, houses, papers and effects against unreasonable seizures and searches shall not be violated; and no warrant shall issue but on probable cause, supported by Oath or Affirmation, particularly describing the place or places to be searched, and the person or persons, and thing or things to be seized.

With slight modification, the language of this section is identical to that of the Fourth Amendment in the federal Bill of Rights. The core of the Fourth Amendment was applied to the states in 1949 (*Wolf v. Colorado*), and the exclusionary rule, prohibiting the use of illegally seized evidence in court proceedings, was made applicable in 1961 (*Mapp v. Ohio*).

In general, a warrant issued by a neutral and detached magistrate upon a showing of probable cause is necessary prior to a search and seizure; however, the federal courts have created a number of exceptions to this rule, including investigatory stops (*Terry v. Ohio*), automobiles (*United States v. Ross*), searches incident to a valid arrest (*Chimel v. California*), voluntary consent (*Cupp v. Murphy*), border crossing searches (*Almeida-Sanchez v. United States*), evidence in plain view (*Coolidge v. New Hampshire*), and when exigent circumstances do not allow time for issuance of a warrant (*Michigan v. Taylor*).

Although this "most precious right" (Attorney General's Opinion 37, March 29, 1919) is now a federal constitutional right applicable to the states, the state courts are frequently called upon to interpret its meaning within the context of state criminal and civil proceedings.

This prohibition has been held to protect guests in a household no less than the home owner, and one need not be personally present at the time of the search to invoke its protections. So long as the individual was "legitimately on the premises when he placed the fruits of the search there," he or she may invoke this protection (*Dean v. Fogliani*).

The protection from unreasonable searches and seizures extends to civil actions, such as the seizure of personal property in a residence for satisfaction of a money judgment (*Luciano v. Marshall*) and searches of business records and documents (Attorney General's Opinion 80, October 18, 1963).

Sec: 19. **Treason**

> Treason against the State shall consist only in levying war against it, adhering to its enemies or giving them Aid and Comfort. And no person shall be

convicted of treason unless on the testimony of two witnesses to the same overt act, or on confession in open court.

The language of this section is virtually identical to that in Article III, section 3 of the U.S. Constitution. It is designed to provide an element of civil liberties protection to dissenters by defining treason narrowly and requiring a heavy burden of proof. The legislature may not define treason any broader than that encompassed by this article although it can, within limits, pass syndicalism and criminal anarchy acts that make using force against the government illegal.

The proof requirements of this section mean that no one can be convicted of treason on circumstantial evidence. There must be a confession in open court (reducing the chances of a coerced confession) or two witnesses to the same overt act. Originally, the 1864 delegates had not included any burden of proof in this section; however, after substantial debate, they agreed that the circumstances when a crime of treason might be levied would be so emotionally and politically charged that special protections would be necessary in order to ensure that individuals were not ruined by malicious political opponents.[7]

This section has not been subject to interpretation.

Sec: 20. Rights retained by people

This enumeration of rights shall not be construed to impair or deny others retained by the people.

The "saving clause" in this section is similar to that in the Ninth Amendment of the U.S. Constitution. It is, perhaps, a measure of symmetry that this is the last section of Article 1, since, like section 1, it is also based on the natural rights and social contract theories of John Locke. Those theories, held by the drafters of the federal and Nevada constitutions, hold that the people retain all rights not surrendered to the government. The federal Bill of Rights and Article 1 of the Nevada Constitution therefore do not confer rights but protect those that the people already possess. Since it is impossible to list all of those rights, this section saves for the people all those rights that they possess but that are not explicitly listed here.

Some of the justices of the U.S. Supreme Court relied on the Ninth Amendment to protect the right to privacy in marriage in *Griswold v. Connecticut*, although more recent interpretations of the right to privacy have relied on the due process clauses of the Fifth and Fourteenth amendments. The Nevada courts could also use this section of the state constitution to protect rights not specifically enumerated, but they have chosen not to do so.

Article 2

Right of Suffrage

At the time of the federal Constitutional Convention in 1787, the qualifications for voting varied widely among states. Although most of the delegates to the Philadelphia convention thought some form of property should be required as a condition of voting, they could not agree on either the amount or kind of property that might meet this requirement. As a result, Article 1, section 2 of the U.S. Constitution leaves to the states the authority to determine the qualifications for voting.

Sec: 1. **Right to vote; qualifications of elector; qualifications of nonelector to vote for President and Vice President of the United States**

All citizens of the United States (not laboring under the disabilities named in this constitution) of the age of eighteen years and upwards, who shall have actually, and not constructively, resided in the state six months, and in the district or county thirty days next preceding any election, shall be entitled to vote for all officers that now or hereafter may be elected by the people, and upon all questions submitted to the electors at such election; *provided*, that no person who has been or may be convicted of treason or felony in any state or territory of the United States, unless restored to civil rights, and no idiot or insane person shall be entitled to the privilege of an elector. There shall be no denial of the elective franchise at any election on account of sex. The legislature may provide by law the conditions under which a citizen of the United States who does not have the status of an elector in another state and who does not meet the residence requirements of this section may vote in this state for President and Vice President of the United States.

As originally ratified in 1864, the Nevada Constitution allowed only white males to vote. The exclusion of blacks seems ironic given that Nevada was born in the midst of the Civil War. However, although the delegates were certainly pro-Union, they were not particularly favorable to equal rights for minorities (see Part I). To the extent that the issue was discussed at all, delegate Nelson E. Murdock perhaps summed up the convention's thinking on the matter best when he stated, "I think the Anglo-Saxon, the Celtic, or any other of the White or Caucasian races, is a far superior race of men to the Indian, the Negro, or any of the colored races. . . . Why should we condescend to make any of the inferior races our equals?"[8]

In response to the ratification of the Fifteenth Amendment to the U.S. Constitution in 1870, section 1 was amended in 1880 to remove the word *white*. In 1914, six years before the ratification of the U.S. Constitution's Nineteenth Amendment, it was amended to include women's suffrage. In 1971 it was amended once more, allowing those between eighteen and twenty years of age to vote.

All fifty states require U.S. citizenship in order to vote, and most require some period of residency in the state. Indeed, the residency requirement generated substantially more debate at the convention than did the racial exclusions. Although this section requires a six-month residency, it is unenforceable (Attorney General's Opinion 85, June 19, 1972) as a result of the U.S. Supreme Court's decision in *Dunn v. Blumstein*, which held that "durational residency requirements" were subject to strict scrutiny as a violation of the right to vote and the right to travel. In its opinion, the Court noted that a thirty-day residency requirement would be sufficient to prevent voter fraud. The state legislature subsequently adopted a thirty-day requirement, but in 1976 the voters inexplicably rejected an amendment to this section that would have created parallel language in the constitution.

The residency provisions of this section have traditionally been read broadly. Residency on an Indian reservation (Attorney General's Opinion 247, September 28, 1926) or military reservation (Attorney General's Opinion 90, August 9, 1932; Attorney General's Opinion 281, March 29, 1946) constitutes residency within the state of Nevada for voting purposes. Similarly, members of the military who reside in Nevada but who came from elsewhere are entitled to vote on the same basis as other state residents (Attorney General's Opinion, April 27, 1972). Students also may establish legal residency in the state for voting purposes "separate and apart from their parents or guardians" if they meet all other "statutory and constitutional requirements of age and residency" (Attorney General's Opinion 48, October 20, 1971).

The 1914 amendment extending suffrage to women removed an original provision that denied the right to vote to anyone who "after arriving at the age of eighteen years shall have voluntarily borne arms against the United States, or held civil or military office under the so-called Confederate States, or either of them, unless an amnesty be granted to such by the Federal Government." The inclusion of this restriction is not surprising given the fact that the convention was meeting in the midst of the Civil War, although some convention delegates objected to it on the principle that Nevada should attempt to reunite the former Confederates with their Union brethren. The debate on whether to include a loyalty oath to the Union, which was to be sworn to by all voters, was "long, angry, and full of twists and turns."[9] A loyalty oath was at first approved, but one week later it was removed in order to gain support for the constitution by former Confederates now residing in the state. During that week, the mining interests had gotten what they wanted on the mine taxation issue and were now seeking to lock up every possible ratification vote. As something of a compromise, however, the legislature is authorized under section 6 of this article to "prescribe by law any other or further rules or oaths" that it might deem necessary.[10]

Because suffrage rules are established by the constitution, the legislature is prohibited from denying, abridging, extending, or changing the qualifications of voters. Thus, any "citizen possessing the qualifications of an elector, as defined and declared in this provision of the Constitution, and who is not disqualified by any of the provisions thereof, is entitled to the right of suffrage" (*State ex rel. Whitney v. Findley*).

Under this section, a "qualified elector" is not synonymous with a "qualified voter" (see Article 15, section 3). Although a person can be required to register to vote, it is not necessary to register in order to be a "qualified elector" (*State ex rel. Boyle v. Board of Examiners*; Attorney General's Opinion 180, April 30, 1918). Anyone meeting the qualifications of this section is considered a "qualified elector" regardless of whether he or she is a registered voter (Attorney General's Opinion 146, February 6, 1956). For electors to be voters, however, they must be registered to vote (Attorney General's Opinion 376, April 25, 1958). The legislature is required to enact voter registration laws in order "to secure in an orderly and convenient manner the right of voting," (*State ex rel. Wilson v. Stone*) but those laws must be "reasonable, uniform, and impartial, and must be calculated to facilitate and secure, rather than to subvert or impede, the exercise of the right to vote" (*State ex rel. Boyle v. Board of Examiners*).

In addition to age, residency, and registration restrictions on the right to vote, section 1 prohibits voting by those who are idiots or insane and those convicted of treason or felony unless restored to civil rights. The former have not been subject to interpretation, and their definitions are unclear. The attorney general has held that, in regard to felons, it is the penalty assessed and not the charge brought against an individual that determines the grade of the offense (Attorney General's Opinion 62, July 29, 1943). Those who have been "honorably discharged from the penalties and disabilities" of their crimes are not removed from the status of a "convicted person," and they are not allowed to vote unless their civil rights have also been restored (Attorney General's Opinion 83-13, September 14, 1983). An individual dishonorably discharged from the military is not allowed to vote if the offense on which the discharge is predicated is a felony under Nevada law (Attorney General's Opinion 72, March 30, 1972). In a California case (*Richardson v. Ramirez*) that is clearly applicable to Nevada, the U.S. Supreme Court upheld the authority of the states to disfranchise felons.

Sec: 2. When residence not gained or lost

> For the purpose of voting, no person shall be deemed to have gained or lost a residence solely by reason of his presence or absence while employed in the service of the United States, nor while engaged in the navigation of the waters of the United States or of the high seas; nor while a student at any institution of learning; nor while kept at any charitable institution or medical facility at public expense; nor while confined in any public prison.

Whether one gains or loses residence in the state is determined by the intent to make the state his or her home and not by mere physical presence (Attorney General's Opinion 220, July 22, 1936). Thus, students, prisoners, and members of the military may be considered residents and entitled to vote by absentee ballot in spite of their physical absence from the state. As noted under section 1, individuals who have come from another state to attend school or serve in the military in Nevada are entitled to residency if they have the intention of making Nevada their domicile (Attorney General's Opinion 276, March 7, 1962).

Sec: 3. Armed forces personnel

> [Repealed in 1972.]

Prior to its repeal, this section stated, "The right of suffrage shall be enjoyed by all persons, otherwise entitled to the same, who may be in the military or naval service of the United States; provided, the vote so cast shall be made to apply to the county and township of which said voters were bona fide residents at the time of their entry into the service; and provided further, that the payment of a poll tax shall not be required as a condition to the right of voting. Provision shall be made by law, regulating the manner of voting, holding elections, and making returns of such elections, wherein other provisions are not contained in this constitution." This section was repealed, and section 2 amended in 1972 to broaden the voting rights of those in the service of the United States.

Sec: 4. Privilege of qualified electors on general election day

> During the day on which any General Election shall be held in this State no qualified elector shall be arrested by virtue of any civil process.

This section, similar to that of most other states, presumably was designed to prohibit government officials from having their opponents or opponents' supporters arrested before they have a chance to vote. It was not debated at the convention and has not been subject to interpretation.

Sec: 5. Voting by ballot; voting in elections by legislature

All elections by the people shall be by ballot, and all elections by the Legislature, or by either branch thereof shall be "Viva-Voce."

This section has not been subject to interpretation.

Sec: 6. Registration of electors; test of electoral qualifications

Provision shall be made by law for the registration of the names of the Electors within the counties of which they may be residents and for the ascertainment by proper proofs of the persons who shall be entitled to the right of suffrage, as hereby established, to preserve the purity of elections, and to regulate the manner of holding and making returns of the same; and the Legislature shall have power to prescribe by law any other or further rules or oaths, as may be deemed necessary, as a test of electoral qualification.

As noted under section 1, the state legislature is required to adopt voter registration rules and is authorized to prescribe voter oaths. The right to vote is an important one and is "not to be taken from the elector upon any doubtful construction of a statute" (*Buckner v. Lynip*). The legislature may not "impose any conditions on the right to registration" beyond those prescribed for electors in the constitution (*Clayton v. Harris; State ex rel. Wilson v. Stone*).

Nevada has adopted a closed primary system; only members of a political party may vote in that party's primary election. Those who have registered "nonpartisan" may vote only in nonpartisan primaries (e.g., state judges) and general elections.

Sec: 7. Poll tax: Levy and purpose

[Repealed in 1966.]

As originally enacted, this section required a poll tax on all males between the ages of twenty-one and sixty, "uncivilized American Indians excepted." This tax stimulated great debate at the convention, with some delegates thinking it too much like a property requirement for voting; nevertheless, it was included in the constitution of 1864. White males had to pay the tax in order to vote; blacks and other minorities were also required to pay the tax, although they were not allowed to vote under the constitution's original section 1. In 1910 this section was amended to eliminate the connection between voting and paying the tax and required the proceeds to go for public roads, but it was never amended to include women although they had been given suffrage in 1914.

The passage of the Twenty-fourth Amendment to the U.S. Constitution in 1964 led the state's voters to repeal this section in its entirety in 1966. At the time of its repeal, the section stated, "The Legislature shall provide by law for the payment of an annual poll tax of not less than two, nor exceeding four, dollars from each male resident in the State between the ages of twenty-one and sixty years (uncivilized American Indians excepted) to be expended for the maintenance and betterment of the public roads."

Sec: 8. Qualifications of voters on adoption or rejection of constitution

All persons qualified by law to vote for representatives to the General Assembly of the Territory of Nevada, on the twenty first day of March A.D. Eighteen hundred and sixty four and all other persons who may be lawful voters in said Territory on the first Wednesday of September next following, shall be entitled to vote directly upon the question of adopting or rejecting this Constitution.

This section established the requirements for voting in the 1864 ratification election and is of historical interest only.

Sec: 9. Recall of public officers: procedures and limitations

Every public officer in the State of Nevada is subject, as herein provided, to recall from office by the registered voters of the state, or of the county, district, or municipality, from which he was elected. For this purpose a number of registered voters not less than twenty-five per cent (25%) of the number who actually voted in the state or in the county, district, or municipality electing said officer, at the preceding general election, shall file their petition, in the manner herein provided, demanding his recall by the people; they shall set forth in said petition, in not exceeding two hundred (200) words, the reasons why said recall is demanded. If he shall offer his resignation, it shall be accepted and take effect on the day it is offered, and the vacancy thereby caused shall be filled in the manner provided by law. If he shall not resign within five (5) days after the petition is filed, a special election shall be ordered to be held within twenty days (20) after the issuance of the call therefor, in the state, or county, district, or municipality electing said officer, to determine whether the people will recall said officer. On the ballot at said election shall be printed verbatim as set forth in the recall petition, the reasons for demanding the recall of said officer, and in not more than two hundred (200) words, the officer's justification of his course in office. He shall continue to perform the duties of his office until the result of said election shall be finally declared. Other candidates for the office may be nominated to be voted for at said special election. The candidate who shall receive highest number of votes at said special election shall be deemed elected for the remainder of the term, whether it be the person against whom the recall petition was filed, or another. The recall petition shall be filed with the officer with whom the petition for nomination to such office shall be filed, and the same officer shall order the special election when it is required. No such petition shall be circulated or filed against any officer until he has actually held his office six (6) months, save and except that it may be filed against a senator or assemblyman in the legislature at any time after ten (10) days from the beginning of the first session after his election. After one such petition and special election, no further recall petition shall be filed against the same officer during the term for which he was elected, unless such further petitioners shall pay into the public treasury from which the expenses of said special election have been paid, the whole amount paid out of said public treasury as expenses for the preceding special election. Such additional legislation as may aid the operation of this section shall be provided by law.

Section 9 on recall was added to the constitution by amendment in 1912 as part of the Progressive era reforms for direct democracy (initiative and referendum are discussed in Article 19). Recall, which exists in twelve states, allows the voters to remove a state or local, but not federal, official from office before his or her term expires (Attorney General's Opinion 225, June 8, 1975). It has never been used against a state official in Nevada and has been generally unsuccessful at the local level as well; thus, there has been little interpretation of this provision.

All public officials in Nevada, except federal officers, are subject to recall, including judges (Attorney General's Opinion 87-7, March 27, 1987). After 25 percent of the number of voters in that unit of government (e.g., state, county, district, township, city) who voted in the last general election have signed a recall petition, the official has five days to resign. If he or she does not, a recall election is held within twenty days, with both sides having an opportunity to state their case on the ballot. Failure to allow the official an opportunity to present his or her justification for actions in office is cause for the election to be declared illegal (Attorney General's Opinion 42, July 14, 1931).

The recall petition need only cite a reason for recall and is not required to give "good" cause, misfeasance, nonfeasance, or malfeasance as a cause for recall; whether the reason is meritorious is "for the electorate to determine" (*Batchelor v. Eighth Judicial District Court ex rel. County of Clark*). Signers of a recall petition are not allowed to withdraw their names once the petition has been filed (Attorney General's Opinion 84, December 31, 1921). The recall election must be a special election and cannot be held as part of a regular election (Attorney General's Opinion B-10, September 17, 1940).

Section 9 allows other candidates to run against the official in a recall election, with the candidate winning the most votes serving out the remainder of the term.

Under the authority granted to it by the last sentence of this section, the legislature has also provided that, where no opponent challenges the official, the ballot will allow voters to vote to recall or not recall an official. If the official is recalled, the office is declared vacant and filled as it would be for any midterm vacancy.

The constitution's recall provisions do guarantee some protection to office-holders from harassment by unsuccessful election challengers and disgruntled voters. An official must have served at least six months before being subject to a recall except for state legislators who are vulnerable after ten days from the beginning of the legislative session after election. The exception for legislators is a result of the fact that the legislature typically meets no more than six months every two years; given that members of the assembly are elected for two-year terms, they would be untouchable by recall without the legislative exception. An additional protection from harassment exists in the requirement that promoters of a second recall election after the failure of the first must pay the expenses of the first recall election prior to any others being held.

Article 3

Distribution of Powers

Sec: 1. Three separate departments; separation of powers

The powers of the Government of the State of Nevada shall be divided into three separate departments,—the Legislative,—the Executive and the Judicial; and no persons charged with the exercise of powers properly belonging to one of these departments shall exercise any functions, appertaining to either of the others, except in the cases herein expressly directed or permitted.

Like the U.S. Constitution, the Nevada Constitution provides for a separation of governmental powers into three branches: legislative, executive, and judicial. In the federal document, however, the doctrine is merely implied; the state constitution adopts it explicitly. The separation of powers required by this article applies only to state government, not to local governments or school districts (Attorney General's Opinion 4, January 26, 1971). Separation of powers is achieved in the Nevada Constitution by two distinct but related methods: separation of duties and separation of personnel.

Separation of Duties

Separation of duties prohibits one branch from performing duties that are the appropriate prerogative of another. The line between these, however, is often blurred, particularly in relation to legislative delegation to the executive branch. The legislature may not delegate its legislative power to another branch of government (*State ex rel. Bull v. Snodgrass*), but it can delegate the power to "determine the facts which will make [a] statute effective" (*Clark County v. Luqman*). In *Luqman*, the legislature was entitled to delegate to the state Board of Pharmacy, an executive branch agency, the ''mere fact finding authority'' to classify drugs into specific schedules.

When delegating its power, the legislature is restricted by Article 3 in that it is required to provide standards ''sufficient to guide the agency with respect to the purpose of the law and the power authorized'' in order to prevent capricious or arbitrary executive action. For example, in *Brennan v. Bowman,* the state supreme court upheld the County Economic Development Revenue Bond Law, which had delegated power to counties to issue bonds for economic development, on the grounds that the delegatory law had established its purpose, the powers of the county, procedures for notice and hearing, the nature and form of the bonds to be issued, investment of revenues, and rights upon default. The specificity of those guidelines would, the court believed, prevent arbitrary or capricious action by the counties in exercising this delegation of power. Thus, the trend has been to interpret the doctrine liberally, with the result of upholding these legislative delegations of power so long as the power to legislate per se is not delegated and the legislature gives specific standards to the agency in the administration of these delegated powers.

The Nevada courts, however, have been very protective of their own prerogatives and have voided several attempts by the legislature to infringe upon the autonomy guaranteed them by the separation of powers. For example, the courts have invalidated legislation mandating judicial action within a fixed period of time (*Waite v. Burgess*), requiring a judge, prior to receiving his paycheck, to file an affidavit showing no cases remain on his docket beyond ninety days (*State ex rel. Watson v. Merialdo*), requiring open meetings of judicial bodies (*Goldberg v. Eighth Judicial District Court ex rel. County of Clark*), diminishing the power of the courts to punish for contempt (*Pacific Live Stock Co. v. Ellison Ranching Co.*), and conferring ministerial duties on judges (*Galloway v. Truesdell*).

At the same time, separation of powers does not preclude executive branch agencies from exercising administrative powers that are quasi-judicial in nature (*Provenzano v. Long*). In *Ormsby County v. Kearney,* the Nevada Supreme Court held that it was constitutionally permissible for the legislature to authorize the state engineer to take evidence and adjudicate water rights because this was not an exercise of judicial power in the constitutional sense. Similarly, in *Nevada Industrial Commission v. Reese,* that court upheld the authority of a commission appeal officer to take evidence and render a decision in contested benefits cases.

Separation of Personnel

Separation of personnel means that no individual may serve in one branch while simultaneously serving in another. Although there has been no major litigation on this issue, the attorney general has been called upon no fewer than fourteen times to provide advisory opinions delineating the appropriateness of such dual appointments.

Members of the legislature may resign to accept an executive appointment provided no other legal impediments exist (Attorney General's Opinion 95, September 28, 1959). However, they cannot simultaneously serve in the legislature and hold an executive branch position, such as a board or commission member (Attorney General's Opinion 212, September 21, 1956), deputy county assessor (Attorney General's Opinion 353, November 24, 1954), director of an executive department (Attorney General's Opinion 183, July 9, 1952), or tax commissioner (Attorney General's Opinion 28, March 12, 1951). Perhaps most important, a state employee (e.g., one who is employed by another branch of government) cannot serve in the legislature even if that individual is given leave without pay to do so (Attorney General's Opinion 357, December 22, 1954). Because the University and Community College System of Nevada (UCCSN) has been held to be a "constitutional corporation" independent of the other branches of government (Attorney General's Opinion 124, April 14, 1964), this restriction has not been held to apply to university or community college professors.

Members of the judicial and executive branches are forbidden to serve in a dual capacity. The attorney general has held, for example, that a justice of the peace cannot serve as a state fish and game commissioner (Attorney General's Opinion 635, June 23, 1948), a member of the county game management board (Attorney General's Opinion 913, April 28, 1950), or a deputy county recorder (Attorney General's Opinion 88, August 1, 1951), all of which are considered to be executive branch positions. Similarly, a mayor cannot serve as a member of the legislature (Attorney General's Opinion 379, April 30, 1958).

Exceptions

The last phrase of Article 3 does make exceptions to the separation of powers doctrine in those "cases herein expressly directed or permitted." Perhaps the most notable exceptions to this doctrine can be found in Article 5, section 17. That provision not only designates the lieutenant governor as president of the senate, with the power of a "casting vote," but also establishes that the president pro-tempore of the senate acts as governor when both the governor and lieutenant governor are disabled or the offices of governor and lieutenant governor become vacant in some other way.

Article 4

Legislative Department

Sec: 1. **Legislative power vested in senate and assembly**

> The Legislative authority of this State shall be vested in a Senate and Assembly which shall be designated "The Legislature of the State of Nevada" and the sessions of such Legislature shall be held at the seat of government of the State.

This section vests the legislative power of the state in the state legislature, which, like all other states except Nebraska, is bicameral. The names *senate* and *assembly* are derived from the California Constitution, on which Nevada's was modeled.

The legislature exercises broad inherent powers beyond those specifically delegated by the state's constitution. "In the legislature rests the entire power of the People, which is neither vested by the People through the Constitution in the executive or judicial departments nor limited by provisions in the Nevada or United States Constitutions" (*Sawyer v. Haydan*). The only limits that apply to the legislature's "plenary power to legislate upon every subject" are those specified by the constitution (*Moore v. Humboldt County*). Absent any specific restrictions, "statutes are to be construed in favor of the legislative power" (*Galloway v. Truesdell*).

As a result of the plenary nature of this legislative power, the remainder of Article 4 primarily represents limitations on that broad power rather than delineating specific grants of power as one finds in the U.S. Constitution's Article I provisions for Congress.

Among other powers, the legislature may establish tax rates (*Matthews v. State ex rel. Nevada Tax Commission*), regulate parole (*Pinana v. State*), define crimes and penalties (*Lapinski v. State*), and even provide by special act for retirement payments to individuals who are not qualified (Attorney General's Opinion 279, June 14, 1957).

As noted under the discussion of Article 3, however, the legislature is prohibited from delegating its legislative power to the federal government (Attorney General's Opinion 17, February 17, 1923) or to members of the executive or judicial branches of the state (*Lapinski v. State; Zale-Las Vegas, Inc. v. Bulova Watch Company*). So long as the power to legislate per se is not delegated and the legislature gives specific standards to the agency, however, the state's courts have been quite liberal in giving great discretion to the legislature even in this area.

The inherent powers authorized by this section include the power of the legislature to refer legislation to the people for a referendum vote. Unlike the popularly initiated referenda provided for in Article 19, however, laws passed in a legislatively initiated referendum can be amended or repealed by the legislature (Attorney General's Opinion 190, May 15, 1975).

Sec: 2. **Biennial sessions of legislature; commencement**

> The sessions of the Legislature shall be biennial, and shall commence on the 3rd Monday of January next ensuing the election of members of the Assembly, unless the Governor of the State shall, in the interim, convene the Legislature by proclamation.

This section has been amended three times: in 1889 to change the starting date of the legislative session from the first Monday to the third Monday of January, in 1958 to provide for annual sessions, and in 1960 to return to biennial sessions.

The 1958 change was later opposed after the attorney general held that the legislature could not limit its even-numbered-year sessions to budget matters only; that would require a constitutional amendment (Attorney General's Opinion 11, February 19, 1959). By initiative, the voters returned biennial sessions in 1960 and later rejected a 1970 amendment returning to annual sessions. As one of the delegates at the 1864 convention noted presciently, "The fact is, that whenever the Legislature is in session, the people wait with fear and trembling for it to adjourn, and then they thank God that it is over."[11]

Sec: 3. **Members of assembly: Election and term of office**

> The members of the Assembly shall be chosen biennialy [*sic*] by the qualified electors of their respective districts, on the Tuesday next after the first Monday in November and their term of office shall be two years from the day next after their election.

There has been no interpretation of this section.

Sec: 4. **Senators: Election and term of office**

> Senators shall be chosen at the same time and places as members of the
> Assembly by the qualified electors of their respective districts, and their
> term of Office shall be four Years from the day next after their election.

Sections 3 and 4 mean that all members of the assembly and approximately half
of the senate are up for election every two years. This structure parallels that of
the U.S. Congress in that it ensures some continuity from one session of the
legislature to the next.

Sec: 5. **Number of senators and assemblymen; apportionment**

> Senators and members of the assembly shall be duly qualified electors in
> the respective counties and districts which they represent, and the number
> of senators shall not be less than one-third nor more than one-half of that
> of the members of the assembly.
>
> It shall be the mandatory duty of the legislature at its first session after
> the taking of the decennial census of the United States in the year 1950,
> and after each subsequent decennial census, to fix by law the number of
> senators and assemblymen, and apportion them among the several counties
> of the state, or among legislative districts which may be established by law,
> according to the number of inhabitants in them, respectively.

Although this section requires only that candidates be "qualified electors," the
legislature has established by statute a minimum age of twenty-one for these
offices (*Mengelkamp v. List*).

Article 15, section 6 establishes a maximum of seventy-five members in the
two houses of the legislature; this section further requires that the number of
senators be no more than one-half nor less than one-third the number of members
of the assembly. The legislature must reapportion in its first regular session after
the decennial census is taken or, if the data are unavailable at that time, in a
special session (Attorney General's Opinion 18, March 15, 1971). The prescribed
number and ratio of senators and assemblymen contained in this section violates
the U.S. Constitution only if "it prevents the adoption of a valid system of
apportionment according to population" (*Dungan v. Sawyer*).

As noted in Part I and the discussions under Articles 1 and 15, this section
was amended in 1950 to make it consistent with the state's practice since 1915
of apportioning senate seats on the basis of one per county. However, since
neither Article 1 nor Article 15 requiring apportionment on the basis of population
was amended, that attempt was of dubious legality. After the decision in *Dungan
v. Sawyer*, this section was amended again in 1970 to provide once more for
apportionment of both houses based on population.

Sec: 6. **Power of each house to judge qualifications of members, choose officers, set rules of proceedings and expel members**

Each House shall judge of the qualifications, elections and returns of its own members, choose its own officers (except the President of the Senate), determine the rules of its proceedings and may punish its members for disorderly conduct, and with the concurrence of two thirds of all the members elected, expel a member.

This section gives the legislature final power to judge the qualifications and elections of its members; its decisions are not subject to review by the courts (Attorney General's Opinion 146, February 6, 1956). Should a member of the legislature accept an executive branch appointment, it is within the sole discretion of the legislature, and not the courts, to determine whether this acceptance constitutes an implied resignation from the legislature (Attorney General's Opinion 183, July 9, 1952).

Sec: 7. **Punishment of nonmember**

Either House, during the session, may punish, by imprisonment, any person not a member, who shall have been guilty of disrespect to the House by disorderly or contemptuous behavior in its presence; but such imprisonment shall not extend beyond the final adjournment of the session.

There has been no interpretation of this section.

Sec: 8. **Senators and assemblymen ineligible for certain offices**

No Senator or member of Assembly shall, during the term for which he shall have been elected, nor for one year thereafter be appointed to any civil office of profit under this State which shall have been created, or the emoluments of which shall have been increased during such term, except such office as may be filled by elections by the people.

This section was added by the convention delegates to prohibit members of the legislature from creating new offices or adding to the salary of existing ones so that they might be appointed to them. Offices that have not been created by the legislature, or for which the legislature has not increased the salary, or which were created more than one year prior to appointment are not covered by this section. Thus, although a legislator cannot, within one year, be appointed to a commission created by the legislature (Attorney General's Opinion 71, October 18, 1921; Attorney General's Opinion 736, April 12, 1949), he or she can serve in an appointed office created by a local housing authority (Attorney General's

Opinion 48, June 7, 1943) or a school district (Attorney General's Opinion 62, May 17, 1955).

A legislator cannot be appointed to an office within one year of his or her term for which the legislature has increased the salary (Attorney General's Opinion 108, October 22, 1951; Attorney General's Opinion 353, November 24, 1954) but may be appointed to an office for which the salary is determined by an executive branch personnel agency (Attorney General's Opinion 280, November 24, 1965).

None of these restrictions applies to elective office. A former senator or member of the assembly may run for any elective office; he or she simply cannot be appointed when the limitations of this section apply (Attorney General's Opinion 151, April 8, 1960).

Sec: 9. Federal officers ineligible for state office; exceptions

> No person holding any lucrative office under the Government of the United States or any other power, shall be eligible to any civil office of Profit under this State; Provided, that Post-Masters [sic] whose compensation does not exceed Five Hundred dollars per annum, or commissioners of deeds, shall not be deemed as holding a lucrative office.

Although this section appears in the state constitution's legislative article, it has been held not to be confined to officers of the legislature. It includes all civil offices of profit in the state. No individual holding federal office on election day is eligible to be elected to these state offices (*State ex rel. Nourse v. Clarke*).

A state officer, whether elected or appointed (*State ex rel. Summerfield v. Clark*), who accepts a federal office effectively resigns from the state office he or she may have held (*State ex rel. McMillan v. Sadler*). These restrictions apply exclusively to civil offices and do not prohibit acceptance of a military commission or office (*State ex rel. Summerfield v. Clark*).

Among the offices held to constitute "civil office[s] of Profit under this State" are the attorney general (*State ex rel. Nourse v. Clarke*), notary publics (*State ex rel. Summerfield v. Clark*), justices of the peace (Attorney General's Opinion, September 1, 1910), state district court judges (Attorney General's Opinion 211, July 31, 1918), and county commissioners (Attorney General's Opinion 109, December 27, 1923).

Sec: 10. Embezzler of public money ineligible for office; disqualification for bribery

> Any person who shall be convicted of the embezzlement, or defalcation of the public funds of this State or who may be convicted of having given or offered a bribe to procure his election or appointment to office, or received a bribe to aid in the procurement of office for any other person, shall be

disqualified from holding any office of profit or trust in this State; and the
Legislature shall, as soon as practicable, provide by law for the punishment
of such defalcation, bribery, or embezzlement as a felony.

A mere charge or indictment of bribery or embezzlement is not sufficient to oust
an individual from office; he or she must be convicted of the offense for the
punishment provided in this section to become effective (*Egan v. Jones*).

Sec: 11. **Privilege of members: Freedom from arrest on civil process**

Members of the Legislature shall be privileged from arrest on civil process
during the session of the Legislature, and for fifteen days next before the
commencement of each session.

This section has not been subject to interpretation.

Sec: 12. **Vacancy**

In case of the death or resignation of any member of the legislature, either
senator or assemblyman, the county commissioners of the county from which
such member was elected shall appoint a person of the same political party
as the party which elected such senator or assemblyman to fill such vacancy;
provided, that this section shall apply only in case where no biennial election
or any regular election at which county officers are to [be] elected takes
place between the time of such death or resignation and the next succeeding
session of the legislature.

This section originally required the governor to issue writs of election to fill
legislative vacancies. It was amended in 1922 and 1944 to its present form,
allowing county commissioners to appoint midterm vacancy replacements so
long as there is to be no regular election between the vacancy and the next
legislative session (Attorney General's Opinion 166, June 21, 1960). The individual who is appointed by the county commissioners will serve only until the
next general election, when the remaining term, if any, will be filled (Attorney
General's Opinion 84, July 18, 1955). Individuals so appointed must not only
be of the same political party as the previously elected official but must also be
from the "district in which the vacancy occurs" (Attorney General's Opinion
5, January 28, 1955).

Sec: 13. **Quorum; compelling attendance**

A majority of all the members elected to each House shall constitute a quorum
to transact business, but a smaller number may adjourn, from day to day

and may compel the attendance of absent members, in such manner, and
under such penalties as each house may prescribe.

There has been no interpretation of this section.

Sec: 14. Journal

Each House shall keep a journal of its own proceedings which shall be
published and the yeas and nays of the members of either house on any
question shall at the desire of any three members present, be entered on the
journal.

This section has not been subject to interpretation.

Sec: 15. Open sessions; adjournment for more than 3 days

The doors of each House shall be kept open during its session, except the
Senate while sitting in executive session, and neither shall, without the
consent of the other, adjourn for more than three days nor to any other place
than that in which they may be holding their sessions.

Many of the delegates at the 1864 convention thought that there should be no
secret meetings of the legislature. A compromise was adopted allowing only
executive sessions of the senate to be held in secret. This section does not apply
to the meetings of legislative committees; thus, the legislature may provide by
its own rules for open and closed committee sessions (*Sarkes Tarzian, Inc. v.
Legislature of State*).

Sec: 16. Bills may originate in either house; amendment

Any bill may originate in either House of the Legislature, and all bills passed
by one may be amended in the other.

The U.S. Constitution gives only the House of Representatives authority to
originate revenue bills. This was part of the Connecticut Compromise and was
included to give the House, based on population and elected directly by the
people, more influence in the taxation process. Neither of these concerns was
applicable in Nevada since both houses were based on population and members
were directly elected; thus, any bill may originate in either house.

Sec: 17. Act to embrace one subject only; title; amendment

Each law enacted by the Legislature shall embrace but one subject, and
matter, properly connected therewith, which subject shall be briefly ex-

pressed in the title; and no law shall be revised or amended by reference to
its title only; but, in such case, the act as revised or section as amended,
shall be re-enacted and published at length.

The provisions of this section are mandatory (*State ex rel. Chase v. Rogers*),
and any act passed in disregard of it is *pro tanto void* (*State v. Ah Sam*). Although
the courts have tended to interpret this section liberally so as not to "thwart
honest efforts at legislation" (*State ex rel. Dunn v. Board of Commissioners*),
they are careful not to extend that construction to "the point of nullification"
(*State v. Payne*).

The major purpose of the convention's delegates in adopting this section was
twofold: to prevent the legislature from passing laws "having no necessary or
proper relation, and which as independent measures could not be carried" (*State
v. Silver*) and to prohibit the legislature from misleading the public through
"innocent" titling of bills "giving no hint of their real nature" (*State ex rel.
Dunn v. Board of Commissioners*).

The "one subject" language of this section does not prohibit a bill from
dealing with "many matters and a multitude of details," but it does require that
these matters be related to "one general subject" (*Southern Pacific Company
v. Bartine*).

The titling requirement exists to "give notice of the subject of the law" (*State
v. Houdley*), and the test of a title under this section is "whether the title is of
such a character as to mislead the public and the members of the Legislature"
(*State v. Payne*). Titles must be specific (*Ex parte Mantell*), and an act cannot
be broader than the "subject expressed in the title" (*State ex rel. Norcross v.
Board of Commissioners*). Statutes that are broader than their titles are invalid
only as to the parts not indicated in those titles (*State ex rel. Abelman v. Douglas*).

Sec: 18. **Reading of bill; vote on final passage; majority necessary to pass bill or joint resolution; signatures; consent calendar**

Every bill, except a bill placed on a consent calendar adopted as provided
in this section, shall be read in sections on three several days, in each House,
unless in case of emergency, two thirds of the House where such bill may
be pending shall deem it expedient to dispense with this rule; but the reading
of a bill by sections, on its final passage, shall in no case be dispensed with,
and the vote on the final passage of every bill or joint resolution shall be
taken by yeas and nays to be entered on the journals of each House; and a
majority of all the members elected to each house, shall be necessary to
pass every bill or joint resolution, and all bills or joint resolutions so passed,
shall be signed by the presiding officers of the respective Houses and by
the Secretary of the Senate and clerk of the Assembly. Each House may
provide by rule for the creation of a consent calendar and establish the
procedure of the passage of uncontested bills.

The delegates to the 1864 convention were generally loathe to legislate specific procedures or rules into the constitution. This section is an exception; it lays out quite specifically the regulations attendant to passage of a bill in the state legislature.

In order to prevent a handful of members from passing legislation in the absence of others, this section requires a majority vote of the total membership in each house, not just those who are present and voting. Currently, passage requires eleven of twenty-one votes in the senate and twenty-two of forty-two votes in the assembly. The attorney general has noted, however, that ''if a bill receives less than such majority vote and the Legislature declares it passed, it is doubtful whether the courts could declare such action unconstitutional'' (Attorney General's Opinion 19, February 10, 1919). Indeed, the Nevada Supreme Court has held that a bill signed by the appropriate officers and deposited with the secretary of state ''must be accepted by the courts . . . as having been regularly enacted by the legislature'' (*State ex rel. Osburn v. Beck*), and the courts ''will not look beyond the statute roll'' for evidence of its passage (*State ex rel. Sutherland v. Nye*).

The bill must be signed by four legislative officials prior to its transmission to the governor: the presiding officers of the two houses, the secretary of the senate, and the clerk of the assembly. These signatures are mandatory; failure to sign means that a bill will not become law, even when it is passed over the governor's veto (*State ex rel. Coffin v. Howell*; Attorney General's Opinion 24, March 25, 1913; Attorney General's Opinion 32, April 1, 1913).

Readings of the bill on three days may be waived when two-thirds of the house votes to suspend the rules. In order to reduce some unnecessary readings on routine matters, this section was amended in 1976 to provide exceptions for bills placed on the consent calendar.

Sec: 19. **Manner of drawing money from the treasury**

> No money shall be drawn from the treasury but in consequence of appropriations made by law.

The government of Nevada is precluded by the terms of this section from spending money that has not been appropriated by the legislature. In this regard, the legislature has virtual plenary power except that it may not appropriate funds to pay claims that have not been presented to the Board of Examiners (see Article 5, section 21) (*Norcross v. Cole*) or use its appropriation power in the abuse of eminent domain (*Heidenreich v. Second Judicial District Court ex rel. County of Washoe*) or in support of sectarian purposes (see Article 11). The appropriations power of the legislature is exclusive (Attorney General's Opinion 126, April 28, 1920); the courts may not order moneys to be paid from the state's general fund (*State v. Second Judicial District Court ex rel. County of Washoe*).

Appropriations bills must pass the legislature in the same manner as other bills (see section 18) and either must be signed by the governor or his or her veto overridden by the legislature in order to be valid (Attorney General's Opinion 85, July 25, 1951). Money that has been validly appropriated for a specific purpose can be used only for that purpose (Attorney General's Opinion 38, June 19, 1931; Attorney General's Opinion B-2, July 22, 1940; Attorney General's Opinion 1, January 4, 1955).

As noted in the discussion under Article 9, section 2, Nevada Industrial Commission and Public Employee Retirement Funds are trust funds that cannot be appropriated by the legislature for other purposes.

Sec: 20. **Certain local and special laws prohibited**

The legislature shall not pass local or special laws in any of the following enumerated cases—that is to say:

Regulating the jurisdiction and duties of justices of the peace and of constables, and fixing their compensation;

For the punishment of crimes and misdemeanors;

Regulating the practice of courts of justice;

Providing for changing the venue in civil and criminal cases;

Granting divorces;

Changing the names of persons;

Vacating roads, town plots, streets, alleys, and public squares;

Summoning and impaneling grand and petit juries, and providing for their compensation;

Regulating county and township business;

Regulating the election of county and township officers;

For the assessment and collection of taxes for state, county, and township purposes;

Providing for opening and conducting elections of state, county, or township officers, and designated places of voting;

Providing for the sale of real estate belonging to minors or other persons laboring under legal disabilities;

Giving effect to invalid deeds, wills, or other instruments;

Refunding money paid into the state treasury, or into the treasury of any county;

Releasing the indebtedness, liability, or obligation of any corporation, association, or person to this state, or to any county, town, or city of this state; but nothing in this section shall be construed to deny or restrict the power of the legislature to establish and regulate the compensation and fees of county officers, to authorize and empower the boards of county commissioners of the various counties of the state to establish and regulate the

compensation and fees of township officers in their respective counties, to
establish and regulate the rates of freight, passage, toll, and charges of
railroads, tollroads, ditch, flume, and tunnel companies incorporated under
the laws of this state or doing business therein.

The plain language of this section suggests by implication that the legislature
has power to pass some special or local laws; it is prohibited from doing so in
the cases specifically enumerated (*McDermott v. Anderson*). This section, along
with Article 8, section 1, was designed to prevent the corruption attendant in
legislatures to giving special favors and benefits to corporations or individuals.
Whereas Article 8 proscribes special privileges for corporations, this section
prohibits the passage of special laws "for the benefit of individuals" (*Evans v.
Job*).

"Local legislation" is that which "operates over a particular locality instead
of over the whole territory of the state"; "special legislation" is that which
"pertains to a part of a class as opposed to all of a class" (*Goodwin v. City of
Sparks*) or "imposes special burdens or confers peculiar privileges upon one or
more persons in nowise distinguished from others of the same category" (*State
v. Consolidated Virginia Mining Company*). Local and special laws are presumed
constitutional by the courts until such time as "facts are presented showing
beyond a reasonable doubt that a general law is applicable" (*Evans v. Job*).

This section does not prohibit the legislature from making reasonable classifications (*State ex rel. Tidvall v. Eighth Judicial District Court ex rel. County
of Clark*). Laws are not required to be applicable to all counties in the state in
order to be "general" laws (*Youngs v. Hall*), but the classifications must be
uniform (*Singleton v. Eureka County*), as must be their application (*County of
Clark v. City of Las Vegas*). Thus, a law that applies only to the state's two
most populous counties is valid so long as "in its operation and effect [it] is so
framed as to apply in the future to all counties coming within its designated
class" (*Reid v. Woofter*). A statute that "attempted to govern elections in a
single, designated county" would be void (*Colton v. Eighth Judicial District
Court ex rel. County of Clark*).

City charters do not fall within the proscriptions of this section; they are given
special protection in Article 8, section 1.

Sec: 21. General laws to have uniform application

In all cases enumerated in the previous section, and in all other cases where
a general law can be made applicable, all laws shall be general and of
uniform operation throughout the State.

Sections 20 and 21 together act as a state version of the equal protection clause
of the U.S. Constitution's Fourteenth Amendment, prohibiting the legislature
from enacting a special or local law "where a general law would be adapted to

the wants of the people or suitable to the just purposes of legislation, or would effect the object thought to be accomplished'' (*Evans v. Job*). It does not prohibit passage of all special or local laws; special laws may be necessary when a general law will not achieve the desired purpose (*Western Realty Company v. City of Reno*).

Whether a general law can be made applicable is a decision that must first be made by the legislature; in reviewing such cases, the courts follow the rule that ''presumptively the decision of the Legislature is correct'' (*Hess v. Pegg*). When a constitutional general law is in conflict with a special law, the courts will resolve the issue ''in favor of the special law'' (*City of Reno v. County of Washoe*).

Regulations that establish and apply uniformly to classifications of individuals or entities are not inherently invalid special laws. The courts will examine such laws on the basis of whether they bear a ''rational relationship'' to a legitimate state objective (*State v. Eighth Judicial District Court ex rel. State*). For example, the legislature may establish population as a criterion for classifying counties or cities (*Anthony v. State*), regulate certain professions such as physicians (*Ex parte Spinney*) or ministers (*Paramore v. Brown*), regulate the broadcast of horse racing information (*Dunn v. Nevada Tax Commission*), require motorcyclists to wear helmets (*State v. Eighth Judicial District Court ex rel. State*), and distinguish between peddlers and solicitors in licensure requirements (*Edwards v. City of Reno*), because each of these classifications is rationally related to a legitimate state purpose.

The ''rational basis'' test is applicable in cases not involving fundamental rights and

involves a three-step inquiry: (1) Does the classification apply alike to all members within the designated class ... (2) Whether some basis in reality exists for reasonably distinguishing between those within and without the designated class, and (3) Whether the challenged classifications have any rational relation to the purposes of the challenged [action]. (Attorney General's Opinion 90-13, October 15, 1990)

Under this test, the legislature may not grant privileges to certain professions and deny them to others similarly situated, such as a grant of immunity to architects and contractors but not others involved in construction projects (*State Farm Fire and Casualty Company v. All Electric, Inc.*). Nor may it deny to those given free transportation the same right to recover for tortious injuries as paying customers (*Laakonen v. Eighth Judicial District Court ex rel. County of Clark*).

In its regulation of local governments, the legislature may pass special acts relating to the incorporation and powers of municipalities (*Western Realty Company v. City of Reno*), but laws that establish county governments or that regulate their internal affairs must ''be general in nature and must apply uniformly throughout the state to all counties similarly situated'' (*County of Clark v. City of Las Vegas*). Thus an act applicable to all counties with a population of more than 200,000 would be valid; an act that regulates the office hours of county officers in a particular county would not (Attorney General's Opinion 244, April 9, 1953).

Sec: 22. **Suit against state**

> Provision may be made in general law for bringing suit against the State as to all liabilities originating after the adoption of this Constitution.

The U.S. Supreme Court's holding in *Chisholm v. Georgia* that a state can be sued in federal court by a citizen of another state led to passage in 1798 of the Eleventh Amendment prohibiting suits in federal court against a state by "Citizens of another State, or by Citizens or Subjects of any Foreign State." That amendment, however, was construed broadly by the Court in *Hans v. Louisiana* to incorporate the doctrine of sovereign immunity and extend to states immunity from suits even by their own citizens. This section authorizes the legislature to waive the state's sovereign immunity in those types of cases in which it chooses to do so; such laws must, however, be of a general and not special nature (*Hardgrave v. State ex rel. State Highway Department*).

Sec: 23. **Enacting clause; law to be enacted by bill**

> The enacting clause of every law shall be as follows: "The people of the State of Nevada represented in Senate and Assembly, do enact as follows," and no law shall be enacted except by bill.

This requirement is mandatory upon the legislature. It is an "imperative mandate of the people in their sovereign capacity" that the legislature "express the authority by which [laws] are enacted." Failure to include all of the words of the enacting clause makes such laws void (*State ex rel. Chase v. Rogers*).

Sec: 24. **Lotteries**

> 1. Except as otherwise provided in subsection 2, no lottery may be authorized by this State; nor may lottery tickets be sold.
>
> 2. The State and the political subdivisions thereof shall not operate a lottery. The legislature may authorize persons engaged in charitable activities or activities not for profit to operate a lottery in the form of a raffle or drawing on their own behalf. All proceeds of the lottery, less expenses directly related to the operation of the lottery, must be used only to benefit charitable or nonprofit activities in this state. A charitable or nonprofit organization shall not employ or otherwise engage any person to organize or

operate its lottery for compensation. The legislature may provide by law for
the regulation of such lotteries.

Because the chief industry of Nevada is gaming, this section would seem to be
out of place in the Nevada Constitution; however, the ban on lotteries has been
narrowly interpreted to exclude the typical casino enterprise: "Although there
is an element of chance in both lotteries and gaming, the evil of lotteries is that
they infest an entire community, where gaming is generally limited to a few
persons or places" (*Ex parte Pierotti*).

Until its amendment in 1990, this section prohibited all lotteries, including
church raffles and charitable door prizes (*State ex rel. Murphy v. Overton; Ex
parte Blanchard*). The 1990 amendment allows charitable institutions to conduct
lotteries and raffles but establishes strict guidelines on their operation.

Sec: 25. **Uniform county and township government**

The Legislature shall establish a system of County and Township Government which shall be uniform throughout the State.

The purpose of this section was to "prevent the adoption of measures proposed
by the representatives of a particular locality, affecting it only, and the state at
large, in relation to county government without particular and careful scrutiny
by the entire Legislature" (*State ex rel. Attorney General v. Boyd*). As such,
the legislature may not single out a certain county (*State ex rel. Attorney General
v. Boyd; Schweiss v. District Court*) or employee (*Moore v. Humboldt County;
Singleton v. Eureka County*) or regulate a single county's business (*Wolf v.
Humboldt County*). It may, however, authorize a single county to issue bonds
for public services (*Buck v. Boerlin; State ex rel. Henderson Banking Company
v. Lytton*) since a general law could not be made applicable.

The legislature does, in fact, distinguish among counties and is allowed to do
so as long as the classifications it makes are "based upon reasonable and actual
differences" and the legislation it enacts is "appropriate to the classification,
and embrace[s] all within the class" (*State ex rel. Attorney General v. Boyd*).
Thus, for example, a law allowing consolidation of city and county law enforcement agencies in city seats having more than 200,000 population was valid,
although at the time it was applicable to only one county and one city, in that
it was "prospectively applicable to all counties which might grow into it, was
rationally related to a legitimate legislative purpose, and was not based upon
any odious, bizarre, or absurd distinctions" (*County of Clark v. City of Las
Vegas*).

Sec: 26. **Boards of county commissioners: Elections and duties**

The Legislature shall provide by law, for the election of a Board of County
Commissioners in each County, and such County Commissioners shall
jointly and individually perform such duties as may be prescribed by law.

The county boards of commissioners are created by the legislature pursuant to
this section, and "their powers are derived exclusively from legislative acts"
(Attorney General's Opinion 88, November 12, 1963). They have no powers
other than those granted by the legislature. They are required to perform such
duties as may be prescribed by law (*State ex rel. Ginocchio v. Shaughnessy*)
and may perform both administrative and quasi-judicial functions as required by
the legislature (*State ex rel. Mason v. Board of County Commissioners*). In
addition, it is within the authority of the legislature to determine the number of
county commissioners (*State ex rel. Copeland v. Woodbury*).

Sec: 27. **Disqualification of jurors; elections**

Laws shall be made to exclude from serving on juries, all persons not
qualified electors of this State, and all persons who shall have been convicted
of bribery, perjury, foregery [*sic*], larceny or other high crimes, unless
restored to civil rights; and laws shall be passed regulating elections, and
prohibiting under adequate penalties, all undue influence thereon from
power, bribery, tumult, or other improper practice.

The legislature is required by the "shall" language of this section to enact such
laws. The section has not been subject to interpretation.

Sec: 28. **Compensation of legislative officers and employees; increase or decrease of compensation**

No money shall be drawn from the State Treasury as salary or compensation
of any officer or employee of the Legislature, or either branch thereof, except
in cases where such salary or compensation has been fixed by a law in force
prior to the election or appointment of such officer or employee; and the
salary or compensation so fixed, shall neither be increased nor diminished
so as to apply to any officer or employee of the Legislature, or either branch
thereof at such Session; Provided, that this restriction shall not apply to the
first session of the Legislature.

In general, the courts have held that changes of compensation that occur during
a term of office are not favored. Any ambiguity will be resolved in favor of
denying the increase (*Cannon v. Taylor*). (See section 33 for restrictions on
legislative pay.)

Sec: 29. **Duration of regular and special sessions**

[Repealed in 1958.]

Prior to its repeal, this section stated, "The first regular session of the Legislature may extend to Ninety days, but no subsequent regular session shall exceed sixty days, nor any special session convened by the Governor exceed twenty days." The experience by 1958 was that this artificial limitation was not reasonable in a legislature that met biennially; however, limits on legislative pay continue to maintain the sixty- and twenty-day limits (see section 33).

Sec: 30. **Homesteads: Exemption from forced sale; joint consent required for alienation; recording of declaration**

> A homestead as provided by law, shall be exempt from forced sale under any process of law, and shall not be alienated without the joint consent of husband and wife when that relation exists; but no property shall be exempt from sale for taxes or for the payment of obligations contracted for the purchase of said premises, or for the erection of improvements thereon; Provided, the provisions of this Section shall not apply to any process of law obtained by virtue of a lien given by the consent of both husband and wife, and laws shall be enacted providing for the recording of such homestead within the County in which the same shall be situated.

This section provides for homestead exemption but leaves the conditions and requirements of it solely to the legislature (*Roberts v. Greer; First National Bank v. Meyers*). Those who do not "substantially comply" with these regulations are not entitled to the exemption (*McGill v. Lewis*).

A lien consented to by both spouses, even for purposes of home improvement, is considered an "obligation" under this section and makes the property vulnerable to seizure and sale for nonpayment (*Commercial & Savings Bank v. Corbett*).

Sec: 31. **Property of married persons**

> All property, both real and personal, of a married person owned or claimed by such person before marriage, and that acquired afterward by gift, devise or descent, shall be the separate property of such person. The legislature shall more clearly define the rights of married persons in relation to their separate property and other property.

This section illustrates the convention's occasional foray into building legislation into the constitution. Although one delegate objected to its inclusion on the basis that he did "not like he-women," there was no real debate on this issue.[12] This section has not been subject to significant interpretation.

Sec: 32. County officers: Power of legislature; election, duties and compensation; duties of county clerks

The Legislature shall have power to increase, diminish, consolidate or abolish the following county officers: County Clerks, County Recorders, Auditors, Sheriffs, District Attorneys and Public Administrators. The Legislature shall provide for their election by the people, and fix by law their duties and compensation. County Clerks shall be *ex-officio* Clerks of the Courts of Record and of the Boards of County Commissioners in and for their respective counties.

This section implies that those constitutional offices that are not named are meant to be excluded from the legislature's power to diminish, consolidate, or abolish. Thus, the legislature cannot, short of a constitutional amendment, consolidate the offices of secretary of state and clerk of the supreme court (*State ex rel. Josephs v. Douglas*). Although this section normally requires the election of these officers, new seats or vacancies can be filled temporarily by other means, such as appointment (*Clarke v. Irwin*).

Sec: 33. Compensation of members of legislature; payment for postage, stationery and other expenses; additional allowances for officers

The members of the Legislature shall receive for their services, a compensation to be fixed by law and paid out of the public treasury, for not to exceed 60 days during any regular session of the legislature and not to exceed 20 days during any special session convened by the governor; but no increase of such compensation shall take effect during the term for which the members of either house shall have been elected Provided, that an appropriation may be made for the payment of such actual expenses as members of the Legislature may incur for postage, express charges, newspapers and stationery not exceeding the sum of Sixty dollars for any general or special session for each member; and Furthermore Provided, that the Speaker of the Assembly, and Lieutenant Governor, as President of the Senate, shall each, during the time of their actual attendance as such presiding officers receive an additional allowance of two dollars per diem.

This section was amended in 1958 concomitant to the repeal of section 29, which had limited the length of legislative sessions. Although the legislature may now meet for any period short of the time of the next session's beginning (see Article 5, section 11), the legislators cannot be paid a salary beyond sixty and twenty days of a general or special session, respectively. They may, however, receive per diem expenses for the entire length of the session.

The legislature establishes its own pay, but members cannot receive any approved increase in that pay until their seats have been up for election. An amendment to eliminate the sixty-dollar cap on postage and stationery expenses was decisively defeated by the voters in 1992. This section has not been subject to significant interpretation.

Sec: 34. **Election of United States senators**

In all elections for United States Senators, such elections shall be held in joint convention of both Houses of the Legislature. It shall be the duty of the Legislature which convenes next preceding the expiration of the term of such Senator, to elect his successor. If a vacancy in such Senatorial representation from any cause occur, it shall be the duty of the Legislature then in Session or at the succeeding Session thereof, to supply such vacancy. If the Legislature shall at any time as herein provided, fail to unite in a joint convention within twenty days after the commencement of the Session of the Legislature for the election [of] such Senator it shall be the duty of the Governor, by proclamation to convene the two Houses of the Legislature in joint convention, within not less than five days nor exceeding ten days from the publication of his proclamation, and the joint convention when so assembled shall proceed to elect the Senator as herein provided.

At the time of the convention in 1864, U.S. senators were chosen by state legislatures. Although this section remains in the constitution, it is probably obsolete by the adoption of the Seventeenth Amendment to the U.S. Constitution in 1913, providing for the direct election of senators.

Sec: 35. **Bills to be presented to governor; approval; disapproval and reconsideration by legislature; failure of governor to return bill**

Every bill which may have passed the Legislature, shall, before it becomes a law be presented to the Governor. If he approve it, he shall sign it, but if not he shall return it with his objections, to the House in which it originated, which House shall cause such objections to be entered upon its journal, and proceed to reconsider it; If after such reconsideration it again pass both Houses by yeas and nays, by a vote of two thirds of the members elected to each House, it shall become a law notwithstanding the Governors [sic] objections. If any bill shall not be returned within five days after it shall have been presented to him (Sunday excepted) exclusive of the day on which he received it, the same shall be a law, in like manner as if he had signed it, unless the Legislature by its final adjournment, prevent such return, in which case it shall be a law, unless the Governor within ten days next after the adjournment (Sundays excepted) shall file such bill with his objections thereto, in the office of the Secretary of State, who shall lay the same before the Legislature at its next Session, in like manner as if it had been returned by the Governor, and if the same shall receive the vote of two-thirds of the members elected to each branch of the Legislature, upon a vote taken in yeas and nays to be entered upon the journals of each house, it shall become a law.

The governor's veto power is somewhat less than that of the president of the United States. The governor has only five days to consider a bill if the legislature is in session and ten days if the legislature has adjourned. Unlike the president, the governor does not have a pocket veto; if he or she fails to sign or veto a bill in the required time frame, it becomes law just as though the governor had signed it.

The required vote to override a gubernatorial veto is also more stringent than that imposed on the U.S. Congress. The state legislature must have a two-thirds vote of the total membership of each house to override, not merely two-thirds of those present and voting.

Like the president but unlike states with a strong executive (e.g., New Jersey), the governor does not have an item veto. That is, a bill must be signed or vetoed in its entirety; he or she cannot pick and choose which parts to sign. This restriction tends not to be as significant as it might be in other states or at the federal level as a result of section 17's requirement that all bills "shall embrace but one subject," thus eliminating the problem of unrelated riders being attached to a nongermane bill in order to gain passage.

The merit of a gubernatorial decision to veto is beyond judicial review. The legislature has sole power to "pass upon that question" through its decision to override (*Birdsall v. Carrick*).

Once the governor has signed a bill and it has been filed with the secretary of state, it becomes law (Attorney General's Opinion, March 13, 1899). A bill vetoed by the governor after the legislature has adjourned must be returned to the secretary of state stating the governor's objections; the legislature must consider the vetoed bill at its next session (Attorney General's Opinion 4, January 23, 1913). All bills, including appropriation measures in the guise of joint resolutions, must be presented to the governor for signature, or they will not become law (Attorney General's Opinion 85, July 25, 1951).

Sec: 36. **Abolishment of county; approval of voters in county**

The legislature shall not abolish any county unless the qualified voters of the county affected shall at a general or special election first approve such proposed abolishment by a majority of all the voters voting at such election. The legislature shall provide by law the method of initiating and conducting such election.

This section, added by constitutional amendment in 1940, has the effect of making county consolidation more difficult. It has not been subject to interpretation.

Sec: 37. Continuity of government in case of enemy attack; succession to public offices; legislative quorum requirements; relocation of seat of government

The legislature, in order to insure continuity of state and local governmental operations in periods of emergency resulting from disasters caused by enemy attack, shall have the power and the immediate duty to provide for immediate and temporary succession to the powers and duties of public offices, of whatever nature and whether filled by election or appointment, the incumbents of which may become unavailable for carrying on the powers and duties of such offices, and to adopt such other measures as may be necessary and proper for insuring the continuity of governmental operations, including changes in quorum requirements in the legislature and the relocation of the seat of government. In the exercise of the powers hereby conferred, the legislature shall conform to the requirements of this constitution except to the extent that in the judgment of the legislature so to do would be impracticable or would admit of undue delay.

This section was added in 1964 during the height of the Cold War, in response, no doubt, to fears of a Soviet first strike. It has not been subject to interpretation.

Sec: 37[A]. Consolidation of city and county containing seat of government into one municipal government; separate taxing districts

Notwithstanding the general provisions of sections 20, 25, 26, and 36 of this article, the legislature may by law consolidate into one municipal government, with one set of officers, the city designated as the seat of government of this state and the county in which such city is situated. Such consolidated municipality shall be considered as a county for the purpose of representation in the legislature, shall have all the powers conferred upon counties by this constitution or by general law, and shall have such other powers as may be conferred by its charter. Notwithstanding the general provisions of section 1 of article 10, the legislature may create two or more separate taxing districts within such consolidated municipality.

As a result of the "special laws" restrictions of sections 20, 25, and 26 and the requirement for resident approval for county consolidation in section 36, a constitutional amendment was necessary to consolidate Carson City and Ormsby

County. It is the first and, to date, only consolidation of a city and county in the state, although Clark County and the City of Las Vegas have, by statute, consolidated their law enforcement entities into a single metropolitan police force (*County of Clark v. City of Las Vegas*).

Executive Department

Sec: 1. **Supreme executive power vested in governor**

> The supreme executive power of this State, shall be vested in a Chief
> Magistrate who shall be Governor of the State of Nevada.

This single sentence accomplishes two goals: It gives executive power to the
chief magistrate and provides the title ''governor'' to that person. Although the
legislative power is a broad one, defined as including all powers that are not
delegated to the executive or judicial branches or prohibited by the U.S. and
Nevada constitutions (see Article 4), the executive power is narrower.

In spite of the generally good relations that Nevada Territory had experienced
under territorial Governor Nye, the delegates generally distrusted executive
power. Thus, unlike governors in states with a strong executive (e.g., New
Jersey), Nevada's governor is not authorized to exercise implied powers and
may exercise only the powers delegated explicitly by the state constitution or
legislative statute (*Galloway v. Truesdell*).

Sec: 2. **Election and term of governor**

> The Governor shall be elected by the qualified electors at the time and places
> for voting for members of the Legislature, and shall hold his office for Four
> Years from the time of his installation, and until his successor shall be
> qualified.

The failed 1863 constitution had provided for a two-year term of office for the
governor. Without debate, the 1864 convention amended this section to a four-
year term. It has not been subject to interpretation.

Sec: 3. **Eligibility; qualifications; number of terms**

No person shall be eligible to the office of Governor, who is not a qualified elector, and who, at the time of such election, has not attained the age of twenty five years; and who shall not have been a citizen resident of this State for two years next preceding the election; nor shall any person be elected to the office of Governor more than twice; and no person who has held the office of Governor, or acted as Governor for more than two years of a term which some other person was elected Governor shall be elected to the office of Governor more than once.

This section originally allowed governors to serve an unlimited number of terms, but it was amended in 1970 to provide a restriction parallel to that on the president of the United States in the Twenty-second Amendment. An individual who served less than two years of the preceding governor's term could be elected to no more than two additional full terms. At most, a governor can serve no more than ten years in that position. This section has not been subject to interpretation.

Sec: 4. **Returns of general election transmitted to secretary of state; canvass by supreme court; declaration of election**

The returns of every election for United States senator and member of Congress, district and state officers, and for and against any questions submitted to the electors of the State of Nevada, voted for at the general election, shall be sealed up and transmitted to the seat of government, directed to the secretary of state, and the chief justice of the supreme court, and the associate justices, or a majority thereof, shall meet at the office of the secretary of state, on a day to be fixed by law, and open and canvass the election returns for United States senator and member of Congress, district and state officers, and for and against any questions submitted to the electors of the State of Nevada, and forthwith declare the result and publish the names of the persons elected and the results of the vote cast upon any question submitted to the electors of the State of Nevada. The persons having the highest number of votes for the respective offices shall be declared elected, but in case any two or more have an equal and the highest number of votes for the same office, the legislature shall, by joint vote of both houses, elect one of said persons to fill said office.

The supreme court acts as the official canvasser of votes in the state. Originally this section applied only to the canvass of votes for state offices; it was amended in 1940 to include federal offices and questions submitted to the voters.

This section and Article 15 section 14 establish that only a plurality, not a majority, is needed for election to these offices. In the rare case of a tie, the legislature is given authority to choose the officeholder.

Should the winning candidate die prior to the election, the losing candidate is not entitled to a certificate of election (*Ingersoll v. Lamb*). Instead, the position would be filled in the normal way, as would any other vacancy in that office. Constitutional amendments become effective upon the canvass of votes by the supreme court (*Torvinen v. Rollins*).

Sec: 5. **Governor is commander in chief of state military forces**

> The Governor shall be Commander in Chief of the Military forces of this State except when they shall be called into the service of the United States.

See the discussion under Article 12.

Sec: 6. **Transaction of executive business; reports of executive officers**

> He shall transact all executive business with the Offices of the Government Civil and Military; and may require information in writing, from the Officers of the Executive Department, upon any subject relating to the duties of their respective Office.

This section has not been subject to interpretation.

Sec: 7. **Responsibility for execution of laws**

> He shall see that the laws are faithfully executed.

In many ways, the governor's responsibilities in this section far outweigh his or her authority. The existence of a plural executive (see section 19) means that other executive officials, such as the attorney general, are independently elected and not accountable to the governor. The independence of elected sheriffs and district attorneys also limits the governor's ability to see that the laws are faithfully executed because these officers are also not accountable to him.

The Nevada Supreme Court has held that the governor cannot refuse or fail to "perform an act clearly required by [the] terms" of a legislative act (*White v. Dickerson*). In enforcing the laws, he must enforce the statutes as they exist (Attorney General's Opinion 60, August 12, 1963).

Sec: 8. **Vacancies filled by governor**

> When any Office shall, from any cause become vacant and no mode is provided by the Constitution and laws for filling such vacancy, the Governor shall have the power to fill such vacancy by granting a commission which

shall expire at the next election and qualification of the person elected to such Office.

In filling vacancies, the governor is freed from the obligation in many other states of seeking legislative approval. This is a practical matter because the legislature meets only about six months every two years and is usually not in session to consider vacancy appointments.

The word *vacant* in this section means "empty"; the governor's appointment power applies equally to new offices as to those vacated by death or resignation (*Clarke v. Irwin*). The governor is, however, limited in this respect. He may replace vacancies only in state, not municipal, offices (Attorney General's Opinion 136, August 14, 1922). The legislature may also require him to share his appointment authority with other executive officers for the filling of some offices, such as railroad commissioners (*Southern Pacific Company v. Bartine*).

By the terms of this section, vacancy appointments are valid only until the next election, at which the remaining unexpired term will be filled.

Sec: 9. Special sessions of legislature; business at special session

The Governor may on extraordinary occasions, convene the Legislature by Proclamation and shall state to both houses when organized, the purpose for which they have been convened, and the Legislature shall transact no legislative business, except that for which they were specially convened, or such other legislative business as the Governor may call to the attention of the Legislature while in Session.

As a result of the infrequent sessions of the legislature, the constitution provides for special sessions when state business cannot await its next biennial meeting. Some states (e.g., Illinois) allow the legislature to call itself into special session, but in Nevada only the governor may do so. This decision to convene a special session is entirely discretionary and not subject to judicial review (Attorney General's Opinion 622, May 21, 1948).

The governor's hand is strengthened in a special session in that the legislature may transact only the business for which it was convened or any other business that the governor may call to their attention during the session "and upon which he may ask legislative action" (*Jones v. Theall*).

This section, along with sections 10 and 11 and Article 4, section 35 granting veto power, give the governor a modicum of power in the legislative process.

Sec: 10. Governor's message

He shall communicate by Message to the Legislature at every regular Session the condition of the State and recommend such measures as he may deem expedient.

Through the State of the State Address, the governor may engage in agenda setting by proposing legislation that he or she would like to see adopted by the legislature. Although an address is required only at the biennial sessions of the legislature, modern governors have often chosen to give an additional one in January of even-numbered years when the legislature does not convene.

This section has not been subject to interpretation.

Sec: 11. Adjournment of legislature by governor

> In case of a disagreement between the two Houses with respect to the time of adjournment, the Governor shall have power to adjourn the Legislature to such time as he may think proper; Provided, it be not beyond the time fixed for the meeting of the next Legislature.

There has been no interpretation of this section.

Sec: 12. Person holding federal office ineligible for office of governor

> No person shall, while holding any office under the United States Government hold the office of Governor, except as herein expressly provided.

Whereas Article 3 prohibits members of the legislative or judicial branches of state government from serving as governor, this section further precludes federal officials from holding the office of governor. It has not been subject to interpretation.

Sec: 13. Pardons, reprieves and commutations of sentence; remission of fines and forfeitures

> The Governor shall have the power to suspend the collection of fines and forfeitures and grant reprieves for a period not exceeding sixty days dating from the time of conviction, for all offenses, except in cases of impeachment. Upon conviction for treason he shall have power to suspend the execution of the sentence until the case shall be reported to the Legislature at its next meeting, when the Legislature shall either pardon, direct the execution of the sentence, or grant a further reprieve. And if the Legislature should fail or refuse to make final disposition of such case, the sentence shall be enforced at such time and place as the Governor by his order may direct. The Governor shall communicate to the Legislature, at the beginning of every session, every case of fine or forfeiture remitted, or reprieve, pardon, or commutation granted, stating the name of the convict, the crime of which he was convicted, the Sentence, its date, and the date of the remission, commutation, pardon or reprieve.

The governor may suspend a fine or forfeiture and grant a reprieve for up to sixty days from the time of conviction. However, this power is quite limited; the governor does not have the authority to do so beyond that time limit and may not remit fines absolutely or grant pardons (*Ex parte Shelor*), powers that are reserved to the state Board of Pardons Commissioners (see section 14), of which he is but one member.

Sec: 14. **Remission of fines and forfeitures; commutations and pardons; suspension of sentence; probation**

1. The governor, justices of the supreme court, and attorney general, or a major part of them, of whom the governor shall be one, may, upon such conditions and with such limitations and restrictions as they may think proper, remit fines and forfeitures, commute punishments, except as provided in subsection 2, and grant pardons, after convictions, in all cases, except treason and impeachments, subject to such regulations as may be provided by law relative to the manner of applying for pardons.

2. Except as may be provided by law, a sentence of death or a sentence of life imprisonment without possibility of parole may not be commuted to a sentence which would allow parole.

3. The legislature is authorized to pass laws conferring upon the district courts authority to suspend the execution of sentences, fix the conditions for, and to grant probation, and within the minimum and maximum periods authorized by law, fix the sentence to be served by the person convicted of crime in said courts.

The delegates at the 1864 constitutional convention agreed that the responsibility for pardoning those convicted of a crime "should not rest upon one man alone."[13] Consequently, this section vests that power in a Board of Pardons Commissioners, consisting of the governor, the attorney general, and the justices of the state supreme court. Unlike the president of the United States, the governor cannot unilaterally grant a pardon. However, he does exercise a veto in this regard in that he must be one of those in the majority to grant a pardon; otherwise no pardon is granted.

This section refers only to pardons, not parole. A pardon "completely frees the offender from the control of the state"; a parole "does not obliterate the crime or forgive the offender," who "remains in the legal custody of the state and under the control of its agents, subject at any time, for breach of condition, to be returned to the penal institution." Consequently, statutes that grant to courts the power to pardon or suspend sentences do not violate this section (*Pinana v. State*). Probation is not a constitutional right; it is, instead, a "privilege legislatively given and is without constitutional implications" (*Shum v. Fogliani*).

Paragraphs 2 and 3 were added by amendment in 1982 and 1950, respectively. Subject to restrictions imposed by the legislature, the State Board of Pardons

Commissioners retains, even under these amendments, the power to commute a sentence of life without possibility of parole to one with the possibility of parole (*Smith v. State*).

Sec: 15. **The great seal**

> There shall be a Seal of this State, which shall be kept by the Governor and used by him Officially, and shall be called "The Great Seal of the State of Nevada."

In fact, the seal is actually kept by the secretary of state. There has been no interpretation of this section.

Sec: 16. **Grants and commissions: Signatures and seal**

> All grants and commissions shall be in the name and by the authority of the State of Nevada, sealed with the Great Seal of the State, signed by the Governor and countersigned by the Secretary of State.

There has been no interpretation of this section.

Sec: 17. **Lieutenant governor: Election, term, qualifications and duties; vacancy or disability during vacancy in office of governor**

> A Lieutenant Governor shall be elected at the same time and places and in the same manner as the Governor and his term of Office, and his eligibility, shall also be the same. He shall be President of the Senate, but shall only have a casting vote therein. If during a Vacancy of the office of Governor, the Lieutenant Governor shall be impeached, displaced, resign, die, or become incapable of performing the duties of the office, or be absent from the State, the President *pro-tempore* of the Senate shall act as Governor until the vacancy be filled or the disability cease.

The 1864 convention delegates did not debate the meaning of the phrase *casting vote*. It is not clear from the debates what this might mean given that Article 4, section 18 requires "a majority of all the members elected to each house" in order to pass a bill or resolution; thus, eleven of the twenty-one senators would have to vote to pass legislation because the lieutenant governor is not an "elected" member of the state senate. Until 1977, lieutenant governors cast votes to break ties on motions or resolutions but not on the final passage of a bill. In that year, the lieutenant governor did vote to break a tie on final passage, but a court challenge was avoided when the bill died in the state assembly.[14]

This section further establishes the line of succession in the absence of the governor: lieutenant governor, president pro-tempore of the senate, and, by statute, speaker of the assembly, and secretary of state.

Sec: 18. **Vacancy in office of governor; duties to devolve upon lieutenant governor**

> In case of the impeachment of the Governor, or his removal from Office, death, inability to discharge the duties of the said Office, resignation or absence from the State, the powers and duties of the Office shall devolve upon the Lieutenant Governor for the residue of the term, or until the disability shall cease. But when the Governor shall with the consent of the Legislature be out of the State, in time of War, and at the head of any military force thereof, he shall continue Commander in Chief of the military forces of the State.

The lieutenant governor may act as governor when the latter is "absent from the State"; however, he may not do so unless there is an "effective absence" and a critical need for action. The governor's absence must be "measured by the state's *need* at a given moment for a particular act" (*Sawyer v. District Court*).

Should a vacancy occur in the office of governor, the lieutenant governor assumes the duties and powers of the governor as acting governor but does not technically vacate the office of lieutenant governor (*State ex rel. Hardin v. Sadler*). He or she is, however, entitled to the salary of the governor (*State ex rel. Sadler v. LaGrave*).

In the case of the disability of the governor, the lieutenant governor acts as governor only until the governor is able to resume duties (Attorney General's Opinion, May 10, 1875).

Sec: 19. **Other state officers: Election, term and qualifications**

> A secretary of state, a treasurer, a controller, and an attorney general, shall be elected at the same time and places, and in the same manner as the governor. The term of office of each shall be the same as is prescribed for the governor. Any elector shall be eligible to either of said offices.

This section originally included the office of surveyor general, but it and section 22 were amended in 1954 to eliminate that position as a constitutional office. Article 5 thus creates six independently elected constitutional offices in the executive branch. Unlike states that have a strong executive, the governor of Nevada cannot appoint the attorney general, secretary of state, and other officers. This "plural executive" arrangement weakens the governor substantially because he has little control over these officials, and they are unaccountable to him. They are frequently members of the other party and may be openly antagonistic to and defiant of the governor. There is, however, little he or she can do, short of using powers of personal persuasion, to control the actions of these officers.

Candidates for these offices must meet the same age and residency requirements as the governor and lieutenant governor, although the plain language of this section would appear to make "any elector" eligible (*State ex rel. Nourse v. Clarke*). Oddly, the attorney general is not required to be a lawyer.

Sec: 20. **Secretary of state: Duties**

> The Secretary of State shall keep a true record of the Official Acts of the Legislative and Executive Departments of the Government, and shall when required, lay the same and all matters relative thereto, before either branch of the Legislature.

The secretary of state is required by this section to maintain records of the legislative and executive branches. This, the section 16 requirement to countersign grants and commissions, and section 21's membership on the Board of State Prison Commissioners and Board of Examiners are the only constitutionally mandated duties of this office. All others are a result of statutes enacted by the legislature pursuant to its authority under section 22.

Sec: 21. **Board of State Prison Commissioners; Board of Examiners; examination of claims**

> The Governor, Secretary of State and Attorney General shall constitute a Board of State Prison Commissioners, which Board shall have such supervision of all matters connected with the State Prison as may be provided by law. They shall also constitute a Board of Examiners, with power to examine all claims against the State (except salaries or compensation of Officers fixed by law) and perform such other duties as may be prescribed by law, and no claim against the State (except salaries or compensation of Officers fixed by law) shall be passed upon by the Legislature without having been considered and acted upon by said "Board of Examiners."

The composition of the Board of State Prison Commissioners was designed to ensure that a "lay board, removed from the difficult problems of prison administration, should review and pass upon the basic rules and regulations in the light of their own experiences, knowledge of public affairs, social conscience and legal expertise" (*Craig v. Hocker*). The power of this board is exclusive and precludes the legislature from altering previous sentences imposed by the courts upon prisoners (*Ex parte Darling*).

The Board of Examiners reviews claims against the state for money or property. The legislature cannot appropriate funds for payment of a claim against the state unless it has first been submitted to the board (Attorney General's Opinion, April

11, 1911). The board cannot, however, review the fixed salaries of officers (*State ex rel. Norcross v. Eggers*) or legislative appropriations for services rendered (*State ex rel. Cutting v. LaGrave*).

The board must present to the legislature all claims that have been filed and for which there has been no appropriation (Attorney General's Opinion 46, May 5, 1959). The actions of the board are subject to review by the state controller, and "the examining powers of both the board and the Controller, with reference to the Legislature, are only advisory" (*State ex rel. Lewis v. Doron*).

Sec: 22. Duties of certain state officers

> The secretary of state, state treasurer, state controller, attorney general, and superintendent of public instruction shall perform such other duties as may be prescribed by law.

Although some duties of the secretary of state are spelled out in the constitution, that is not true for the other four constitutional officers. However, it has been determined that the controller may exercise the "recognized duties appurtenant to such office," including "final auditing and settling of all claims against the state" (*State ex rel. Lewis v. Doron*).

The attorney general has no constitutionally prescribed duties, and whatever powers may be exercised are to be found only in the statutes (*Ryan v. Eighth Judicial District Court ex. rel. County of Clark*).

Judicial Department

Sec: 1. **Judicial power vested in court system**

> The Judicial power of this State shall be vested in a court system, comprising a Supreme Court, District Courts, and Justices of the Peace. The Legislature may also establish, as part of the system, Courts for municipal purposes only in incorporated cities and towns.

Article 6 vests the judicial power, interpreted as meaning, with Article 3's declaration of separation of powers, that the courts' power is exclusive and that "neither the legislative nor the executive branches of the government may assume to exercise any part of the judicial power, and the . . . courts cannot be directed, controlled, or impeded in their functions by either of those branches" (*State ex rel. Watson v. Merialdo*).

Included within the judicial power is not only "the authority to hear and determine" but also "the power to decide finally and conclusively, and also the power to carry [the courts'] determination into effect" (*Bergman v. Kearney; Galloway v. Truesdell*). This includes the power of judicial review. Regulation and licensing of attorneys and the promulgation of court rules are within the judicial power and to be exercised solely by the courts (*Galloway v. Truesdell*).

Under this section and the doctrine of separation of powers, the powers of the courts are limited; they can exercise only judicial powers and cannot be delegated powers or functions that are legislative or executive in character, such as assessing and equalizing property (*Sawyer v. Dooley*) or fixing railroad rates (*Southern Pacific Company v. Bartine*).

Section 1 establishes a three-tiered set of courts in the state: supreme court, courts of general jurisdiction, and courts of limited jurisdiction. Justice courts, staffed by justices of the peace, are courts of limited jurisdiction hearing only minor criminal and civil cases. In addition, the legislature has created municipal courts as courts of limited jurisdiction in incorporated areas.

The district courts serve as courts of general jurisdiction and hear criminal and civil matters more serious than those handled at the justice court level. The Nevada Supreme Court is the court of last resort except in cases involving a federal issue; in such cases, final appeal may be taken to the U.S. Supreme Court.

Nevada is one of only a few states without an intermediate court of appeals. In 1972, 1980, and 1992, voters rejected legislatively proposed constitutional amendments to this section creating an intermediate court.

Sec: 2. Supreme Court: Composition; staggered terms of justices; holding of court by panels of justices and full court

1. The supreme court consists of the chief justice and two or more associate justices, as may be provided by law. In increasing or diminishing the number of associate justices, the legislature shall provide for the arrangement of their terms so that an equal number of terms, as nearly as may be, expire every 2 years.

2. The legislature may provide by law:

(a) If the court consists of more than five justices, for the hearing and decision of cases by panels of no fewer than three justices, the resolution by the full court of any conflicts between decisions so rendered, and the kinds of cases which must be heard by the full court.

(b) For the places of holding court by panels of justices if established, and by the full court.

This section was the subject of great debate at the convention. Given the perceived corruption of the territorial judiciary, the delegates expended great effort to maintain an honest state bench. Although some argued that five justices would be harder to bribe than three, others were concerned that it would be difficult to find five "pure" and "able" justices to sit on the high court.[15] Eventually, a compromise was adopted setting the number at three, with legislative authorization to increase the number to five without a constitutional amendment. That expansion took place in 1967.

In 1976 this section was amended to remove the cap on the number of justices on the court, leaving the issue entirely to the legislature. Should the legislature choose to increase the number beyond five, it must continue to provide for staggered terms (see section 3) and may provide for the court to hear cases in panels of three or more, as is currently done in U.S. Courts of Appeals. This section has not been subject to significant interpretation.

Sec: 3. **Justices of supreme court: Election; terms; chief justice**

The Justices of the Supreme Court, shall be elected by the qualified electors
of the State at the general election, and shall hold office for the term of Six
Years from and including the first Monday of January next succeeding their
election; Provided, that there shall be elected, at the first election under this
Constitution, Three Justices of the Supreme Court who shall hold Office
from and including the first Monday of December AD. Eighteen hundred
and Sixty four, and continue in Office thereafter, Two, Four and Six Years
respectively, from and including the first Monday of January next suceeding
[*sic*] their election. They shall meet as soon as practicable after their election
and qualification, and at their first meeting shall determine by lot, the term
of Office each shall fill, and the Justice drawing the shortest term shall be
Chief Justice, and after the expiration of his term, the one having the next
shortest term shall be Chief Justice, after which the Senior Justice in Commission shall be Chief Justice; and in case the commission of any two or
more of said Justices shall bear the same date, they shall determine by lot,
who shall be Chief Justice.

Thirty-one states, including Nevada, elect all or some of their state judges.[16]
Given its history with appointed territorial judges, it is not at all surprising that
Nevada chose the election method. Until 1915, these elections were partisan (a
candidate was identified by political party), but in 1915 the state legislature made
all judicial offices nonpartisan. Nevertheless, since 1916, 57 percent of supreme
court justices in Nevada have initially attained the bench not by election but
through gubernatorial appointment to fill midterm vacancies.[17]

Supreme Court justices serve six-year, staggered terms. The chief justiceship
is not an elected position; the justice with the least amount of service remaining
on his or her term of office serves as chief justice. When two or more justices
have an equal amount of their terms remaining, the chief justiceship is determined
by lot (typically a coin toss). A proposed constitutional amendment to have the
court elect its chief justice from among its members was defeated by the voters
in 1992.

Sec: 4. **Jurisdiction of supreme court; appointment of district judge to sit for disabled or disqualified justice**

The supreme court shall have appellate jurisdiction in all civil cases arising
in district courts, and also on questions of law alone in all criminal cases
in which the offense charged is within the original jurisdiction of the district
courts. The court shall also have power to issue writs of *mandamus, certiorari,* prohibition, *quo warranto,* and *habeas corpus* and also all writs
necessary or proper to the complete exercise of its appellate jurisdiction.
Each of the justices shall have power to issue writs of *habeas corpus* to any
part of the state, upon petition by, or on behalf of, any person held in actual

custody, and may make such writs returnable, before himself or the supreme court, or before any district court in the state or before any judge of said courts.

In case of the disability or disqualification, for any cause, of the chief justice or one of the associate justices of the supreme court, or any two of them, the governor is authorized and empowered to designate any district judge or judges to sit in the place or places of such disqualified or disabled justice or justices, and said judge or judges so designated shall receive their actual expense of travel and otherwise while sitting in the supreme court.

The Nevada Supreme Court exercises both appellate and original jurisdiction; however, most of its caseload is appellate, since its original jurisdiction is limited to the writs listed in section 4 (*Curtis v. McCullough*).

The court has "no jurisdiction other than that expressly stated" (*Lake v. Lake*), and the legislature has no authority to increase the original jurisdiction established by this section (Attorney General's Opinion 23, March 25, 1913). Cases originally decided in the district courts are appealable to the supreme court (*Klein v. Allenbach*), but those initiated in the courts of limited jurisdiction and then appealed to the district courts are not.

The Nevada Constitution does not include the "cases and controversies" language of the U.S. Constitution, but there still exist a number of constitutionally and self-imposed restrictions on the supreme court's ability to hear appeals. Like the federal courts, the Nevada Supreme Court will not give advisory opinions (*City of North Las Vegas v. Cluff*) and will not decide moot questions (*Boulet v. City of Las Vegas*). Nor is the legislature empowered to expand the court's appellate jurisdiction beyond this section to authorize it to hear moot questions (*State v. Viers*).

The "questions of law alone" language in this section restricts the court in criminal cases to the resolution of questions of law only, not questions of fact. The court cannot "disturb the trial court's factual finding in criminal cases" (*State v. Busscher*). However, as a question of law, the court can determine "whether the evidence is sufficient to sustain" a guilty verdict (*State v. Van Winkle; State v. Wilson*) or "whether the evidence is sufficient to show the commission of a crime" (*State v. Busscher*).

When a justice is disabled or disqualified from hearing a case, the governor is authorized to appoint a district judge to sit in his or her place.[18] Typically, the court itself suggests an individual to the governor, who then makes the appointment.

Sec: 5. Judicial districts; election and terms of district judges

The state is hereby divided into Nine Judicial Districts of which the county of Storey shall constitute the First; The county of Ormsby the Second; The county of Lyon the Third; The county of Washoe the Fourth; The counties of Nye and Churchill the Fifth; The county of Humboldt the Sixth; The county of Lander the Seventh; The county of Douglas the Eighth; and the county of Esmeralda the Ninth. The county of Roop shall be attached to the county of Washoe for judicial purposes until otherwise provided by law. The Legislature may, however, provide by law for an alteration in the boundaries or divisions of the Districts herein prescribed, and also for increasing or diminishing the number of the Judicial Districts and Judges therein. But no such change shall take effect, except in case of a vacancy, or the expiration of the term of an incumbent of the Office. At the first general election under this Constitution there shall be elected in each of the respective Districts (except as in this Section hereafter otherwise provided) One District Judge, who shall hold Office from and including the first Monday of January in the year Eighteen hundred and Sixty four and until the first Monday of January in the year Eighteen hundred and Sixty seven. After the said first election, there shall be elected at the General election which immediately precedes the expiration of the term of his predecessor, One District Judge in each of the respective Judicial Districts (except in the First District as in this Section hereinafter provided.) The District Judges shall be elected by the qualified electors of their respective districts, and shall hold office for the term of 6 years (excepting those elected at said first election) from and including the first Monday of January, next succeeding their election and qualification; Provided that the First Judicial District shall be entitled to, and shall have Three District Judges, who shall possess co-extensive and concurrent jurisdiction, and who shall be elected at the same times, in the same manner, and shall hold office for the like terms as herein prescribed, in relation to the Judges in other Judicial Districts, any one of said Judges may preside on the empanneling [*sic*] of Grand Juries and the presentment and trial on indictments, under such rules and regulations as may be prescribed by law.

Most of this section is of historical interest only in that it set up the original division of the state into judicial districts. The legislature is given the authority to change these districts and has done so many times since 1864—there have been nine districts since 1973. Although district courts are single-judge courts, a single district may have more than one judge. Like supreme court justices, district court judges are selected in nonpartisan elections for six-year terms of office. Unlike these justices, however, this section prohibits them from serving staggered terms, so all district court judgeships in the state come up for election at the same time (*State ex rel. Hubbard v. Gorin*).

The legislature's power to alter, increase, or diminish the number of judicial districts and district court judges is virtually unlimited. It may alter old districts or form new judicial districts (*State ex rel. Leake v. Blasdel*) and may even establish the entire state as a single judicial district (*State ex rel. Coffin v. County Commissioners*). Once a district has been created, however, the term *diminish* in this section does not allow the legislature to deprive a district totally of a judge (*State ex rel. Aude v. Kinkead*).

In addition to the jurisdiction of district courts established by section 6 of this article, the judges of these courts exercise "reasonable judicial control of grand juries" through empanelment of grand juries and the presentment and trial of indictments (*In re Report of Washoe County Grand Jury*). That power is a general one, not limited by statute, to ensure that "the grand jury and its process are not abused, or used for purposes of oppression and injustice" (*Lane v. Second Judicial District Court*).

The power of the legislature is further restricted in that it cannot diminish the number of judges in a district unless there is a vacancy or the term of the judge has expired. This provision, along with section 15's prohibition on salary diminution, was designed to achieve a limited measure of judicial independence by "ensure[ing] the security of district judges during their term of office." Newly created judgeships can, however, be filled in the usual manner (see section 20) without need for a vacancy or term expiration (*Second Judicial District State Bar v. List*).

Sec: 6. District courts: Jurisdiction; referees; family court

1. The District courts in the several Judicial Districts of this State have original jurisdiction in all cases excluded by law from the original jurisdiction of justices' courts. They also have final appellate jurisdiction in cases arising in Justices Courts and such other inferior tribunals as may be established by law. The District Courts and the Judges thereof have power to issue writs of Mandamus, Prohibition, Injunction, Quo-Warranto, Certiorari, and all other writs proper and necessary to the complete exercise of their jurisdiction. The District Courts and the judges thereof shall also have power to issue writs of Habeas Corpus on petition by, or on behalf of any person who is held in actual custody in their respective districts, or who has suffered a criminal conviction in their respective districts and has not completed the sentence imposed pursuant to the judgment of conviction.

2. The Legislature may provide by law for:

(a) Referees in district courts.

(b) The establishment of a family court as a division of any district court and may prescribe its jurisdiction.

District courts exercise both original and appellate jurisdiction. Their original jurisdiction is broad and includes all cases in which the legislature has not granted jurisdiction to the justice and municipal courts (*Moore v. Orr; K.J.B. Inc. v. Second Judicial District Court ex rel. County of Washoe*). Appeals from the final orders or decisions of state administrative agencies (e.g., Industrial Commission, Gaming Control Board) are heard by the district courts as part of their original (not appellate) jurisdiction even though these agencies are not mentioned in the state's constitution (*Nevada Industrial Commission v. Reese; Nevada Tax*

Commission v. Mackie; State Gaming Control Board v. Eighth Judicial District Court ex rel. County of Clark).

The appellate jurisdiction of the district courts entails the hearing of appeals from the justice and municipal courts. Because the latter two are not courts of record, by statute appeals to the district court are tried *de novo*; that is, a new trial is held, with the usual witnesses, testimony, evidence, and so forth. Appeals to the district court are final; thus, cases originating in the justice and municipal courts cannot be appealed to the Nevada Supreme Court (*Tripp v. City of Sparks*). Because the district courts have "equal and coextensive jurisdiction," they cannot review, vacate, or direct the actions of other district courts (*Warden, Nevada State Prison v. Owens; Rohlfing v. Second Judicial District Court ex rel. County of Washoe*).

Prior to 1992 an inmate had the option of seeking a writ of habeas corpus from the court in the district in which he or she was being held or in the district court of conviction. However, a 1992 amendment allows the legislature to establish, by statute, the availability of habeas corpus only in the district court of conviction, thus reducing the burden on courts in the (often rural) districts where state prisons are located.

A 1990 amendment authorizes the legislature to create family court divisions in the district courts for the purpose of hearing domestic law cases such as child custody, divorces, and so forth. The legislature exercised that authority in 1991, and the family court judges were first chosen in the 1992 elections.[19]

Sec: 7. **Terms of court**

> The times of holding the Supreme Court and District Courts shall be as fixed by law. The terms of the Supreme Court shall be held at the seat of Government unless the Legislature otherwise provides by law, except that the Supreme Court may hear oral argument at other places in the state. The terms of the District Courts shall be held at the County seats of their respective counties; Provided, that in case any county shall be hereafter divided into two or more districts, the Legislature may by law, designate the places of holding Courts in such Districts.

Although this section originally restricted the supreme court to hearing cases only in Carson City, a pair of 1976 amendments authorized the legislature to establish other places for holding court and to allow cases to be heard outside the state capital. The court does, in fact, frequently hear cases in Las Vegas, which, as the state's population center, generates a substantial number of appeals. This section has not been subject to significant interpretation.

Sec: 8. **Number, qualifications, terms of office and jurisdiction of justices of the peace; appeals; courts of record**

The Legislature shall determine the number of Justices of the Peace to be elected in each city and township of the State, and shall fix by law their qualifications, their terms of office and the limits of their civil and criminal jurisdiction, according to the amount in controversy, the nature of the case, the penalty provided, or any combination of these.

The provisions of this section affecting the number, qualifications, terms of office and jurisdiction of Justices of the Peace become effective on the first Monday of January, 1979.

The Legislature shall also prescribe by law the manner, and determine the cases in which appeals may be taken from Justices and other courts. The Supreme Court, the District Courts, and such other Courts, as the Legislature shall designate, shall be Courts of Record.

Justice courts in Nevada are courts of limited jurisdiction (*Paul v. Armstrong*), and the legislature has authority to determine that jurisdiction. In addition, the legislature has exclusive authority to establish the number of justices of the peace (*State ex rel. Bull v. Snodgrass*).

Justices of the peace are required by this section to be elected (*State ex rel. Bull v. Snodgrass*); however, the legislature is free to establish their terms of office (currently four years).

The supreme court and district courts are required to be courts of record. By implication, this section means that justice courts are not; consequently, appeals from these courts to the district courts are required by statute to be heard *de novo*.

Sec: 9. **Municipal courts**

Provision shall be made by law prescribing the powers, duties and responsibilities of any Municipal Court that may be established in pursuance of Section One, of this Article; and also fixing by law the jurisdiction of said Court so as not to conflict with that of the several courts of Record.

Although the legislature is not required to establish municipal courts, once it does so these courts "exist as a coequal branch of local government within the . . . judicial system" of the state (*City of North Las Vegas ex rel. Arndt v. Daines*).

The power of the legislature to establish the jurisdiction of these courts is limited in several respects. They cannot exercise jurisdiction that conflicts with that of the courts of record (Attorney General's Opinion 561, January 20, 1948); they are restricted by section 1 to hearing only cases of a municipal nature (*Meagher v. County of Storey*); and they lack the authority to determine the constitutionality of statutes or ordinances (*Ex parte Dixon*).

Sec: 10. **Fees or perquisites of judicial officers**

No Judicial Officer, except Justices of the Peace and City Recorders shall
receive to his own use any fees or perquisites of Office.

There has been no significant interpretation of this section.

Sec: 11. **Justices and judges ineligible for other offices**

The justices of the supreme court and the district judges shall be ineligible
to any office, other than a judicial office, during the term for which they
shall have been elected or appointed; and all elections or appointments of
any such judges by the people, legislature, or otherwise, during said period,
to any office other than judicial, shall be void.

As originally ratified, this restriction applied only to elected judges (Attorney
General's Opinion 287, April 11, 1946); however, a 1950 amendment extended
it to appointed judges as well.

The terms of this section do not prohibit judges from resigning to run for
federal office (*State ex rel. Santini v. Swackhamer*), *nor do they apply to justices
of the peace (Attorney General's Opinion 672, July 10, 1970).*

Sec: 12. **Judges not to charge jury respecting matters of fact**

Judges shall not charge juries in respect to matters of fact, but may state
the testimony and declare the law.

The purpose of this section is to "remove the jury beyond the reach of any
influence of the judge in the determination of all issues of fact" (*State v. Duffy*)
and to provide a barrier between judge and jury that will ensure the freedom of
the "jury to decide facts and the reasonable inferences therefrom" without
interference from the court (*Wheeler v. Twin Lakes Riding Stable, Inc.*)

Judges may not, under the restrictions imposed here, charge juries "in respect
to matters of fact," comment on the "probability or improbability of the truth
of the evidence" (*Wheeler v. Twin Lakes Riding Stable, Inc.; Gordon v. Hurtado*) or the credibility of witnesses (*Graves v. State*), volunteer an opinion on
material facts in the course of deciding a question of law (*State v. Harkin*),
provide instructions that assume a fact in dispute (*State v. Buralli*), comment
on the credibility of a defendant (*Graves v. State*), or express an opinion on a
defendant's guilt (*Ex parte Smith*). However, judges may restate testimony (*State
v. Smith, 1875; Bostic v. State*), point out contradictions in testimony (*State v.
McLane*), and instruct a jury that it is "the ultimate judge of the weight and
worth of the evidence" (*Milligan v. State*).

Violations of this section constitute reversible error if they are "prejudicial or improper" (*State v. Loveless; State v. Harkin*) but not if the error is harmless (*Gordon v. Hurtado*).

Sec: 13. Style of process

The style of all process shall be "The State of Nevada" and all prosecutions shall be conducted in the name and by the authority of the same.

Violations of municipal ordinances may be brought in the name of the city rather than the state (*Williams v. Municipal Judge of the City of North Las Vegas*).

Sec: 14. One form of civil action

There shall be but one form of civil action, and law and equity may be administered in the same action.

There has been no significant interpretation of this section.

Sec: 15. Compensation of judges

The Justices of the Supreme Court and District Judges shall each receive for their services a compensation to be fixed by law and paid in the manner provided by law, which shall not be increased or diminished during the term for which they shall have been elected, unless a Vacancy occurs, in which case the successor of the former incumbent shall receive only such salary as may be provided by law at the time of his election or appointment; and provision shall be made by law for setting apart from each year's revenue a sufficient amount of Money, to pay such compensation.

As a companion to section 5's prohibition on diminishing the number of judges absent a vacancy or end of term, this section provides for a measure of judicial independence by protecting judicial salaries from diminution or increase during a term of office. Any statute made effective during a judge's term that increases, diminishes, or completely deprives him or her of compensation violates this section (Attorney General's Opinion, July 5, 1909).

Sec: 16. Special fee in civil action for compensation of judges

The Legislature at its first Session, and from time to time thereafter shall provide by law, that upon the institution of each civil action, and other proceedings, and also upon the perfecting of any appeal in any civil action or proceeding, in the several Courts of Record in this State, a special Court fee, or tax shall be advanced to the Clerks of said Courts, respectively by the party or parties bringing such action or proceeding, or taking such appeal and the money so paid in shall be accounted for by such Clerks, and applied towards the payment of the compensation of the Judges of said Courts, as shall be directed by law.

This section makes the courts somewhat self-sufficient in that court fees that are "reasonable and nondiscriminatory" are used for judges' compensation. These fees, however, are not "intended to assume the whole burden of compensation of judges" and must bear a "reasonable relation to the value of the services rendered." Fees that are so extraordinary as not to bear a reasonable relation are nothing more than impermissible taxes on the right to bring a lawsuit (Attorney General's Opinion 425, February 28, 1947).

Sec: 17. Absence of judicial officer from state; vacation of office

The Legislature shall have no power to grant leave of absence to a Judicial Officer, and such Officer who shall absent himself from the State for more than Ninety consecutive days, shall be deemed to have vacated his Office.

There has been no interpretation of this section.

Sec: 18. Territorial judicial officers not superseded until election and qualification of successors

No Judicial Officer shall be superceeded [sic] nor shall the Organization of the several Courts of the Territory of Nevada be changed until the election and qualification of the several Officers provided for in this article.

This provision is of historical interest only as a method of ensuring a smooth transition from the territorial to state judiciary.

Sec: 19. Administration of court system by chief justice

1. The chief justice is the administrative head of the court system. Subject to such rules as the supreme court may adopt, the chief justice may:

(a) Apportion the work of the supreme court among the justices.

(b) Assign district judges to assist in other judicial districts or to specialized functions which may be established by law.

(c) Recall to active service any retired justice or judge of the court system who consents to such recall and who has not been removed or retired for cause or defeated for retention in office, and may assign him to appropriate temporary duty within the court system.

2. In the absence or temporary disability of the chief justice, the associate justice senior in commission shall act as chief justice.

3. This section becomes effective July 1, 1977.

This section was added by constitutional amendment in 1976 to provide for a unified court structure in the state with the chief justice of the Nevada Supreme Court as its administrative head.

In 1991, a majority of the supreme court adopted Rule 7, institutionalizing the position of vice chief justice implicitly provided for in paragraph 2 of this section and which had existed by custom for some time. The vice chief justice acts as chief justice when the latter is "absent from the court, disqualified, mentally, emotionally and physically disabled, or otherwise unavailable."[20]

As administrative head of the state's court system, the supreme court, through the chief justice, has the inherent power to "take actions reasonably necessary to administer justice efficiently, fairly, and economically" (*In re Dunleavy*). In this capacity, the court may conduct inquiries and take any action necessary, short of removing a judge from office (*Goldman v. Bryan*), including the reassignment of a case when the judge "cannot fairly deal with the matters involved" (*Wickliffe v. Sunrise Hospital*).

Sec: 20. Commission on judicial selection

1. When a vacancy occurs before the expiration of any term of office in the supreme court or among the district judges, the governor shall appoint a justice or judge from among three nominees selected for such individual vacancy by the commission on judicial selection.

2. The term of office of any justice or judge so appointed expires on the first Monday of January following the next general election.

3. Each nomination for the supreme court shall be made by the permanent commission, composed of:

(a) The chief justice or associate justice designated by him;

(b) Three members of the State Bar of Nevada, a public corporation created by statute, appointed by its board of governors; and

(c) Three persons, not members of the legal profession, appointed by the governor.

4. Each nomination for the district court shall be made by a temporary commission composed of:

(a) The permanent commission;

(b) A member of the State Bar of Nevada resident in the judicial district in which the vacancy occurs, appointed by the board of governors of the State Bar of Nevada; and

(c) A resident of such judicial district, not a member of the legal profession, appointed by the governor.

5. If at any time the State Bar of Nevada ceases to exist as a public corporation or ceases to include all attorneys admitted to practice before the courts of this state, the legislature shall provide by law, or if it fails to do so the court shall provide by rule, for the appointment of attorneys at law to the positions designated in this section to be occupied by members of the State Bar of Nevada.

6. The term of office of each appointive member of the permanent commission, excepting the first members, is 4 years. Each appointing authority shall appoint one of the members first appointed for a term of 2 years. If a vacancy occurs, the appointing authority shall fill the vacancy for the unexpired term. The additional members of a temporary commission shall be appointed when a vacancy occurs, and their terms shall expire when the nominations for such vacancy have been transmitted to the governor.

7. An appointing authority shall not appoint to the permanent commission more than:

(a) One resident of any county.

(b) Two members of the same political party.

No member of the permanent commission may be a member of a commission on judicial discipline.

8. After the expiration of 30 days from the date on which the commission on judicial selection has delivered to him its list of nominees for any vacancy, if the governor has not made the appointment required by this section, he shall make no other appointment to any public office until he has appointed a justice or judge from the list submitted. If a commission on judicial selection is established by another section of this constitution to nominate persons to fill vacancies on the supreme court, such commission shall serve as the permanent commission established by subsection 3 of this section.

Although the state's voters rejected the merit selection of judges in 1972 and 1988, they did adopt this section in 1976 creating a modified merit system for the filling of midterm vacancies on the district courts and supreme court. This amendment had the effect of removing what had previously been the governor's sole discretion to fill judicial vacancies. He must now select from a list of three names given to him by the commission.

This system modifies the typical merit system in several ways. First, this is not the normal method of filling judicial posts; it is used only in the case of a midterm vacancy. Second, the judge who is appointed by the governor serves only until the next general election. At that time he or she must run for the remainder of the unexpired term in a nonpartisan election against any opponents who may file and not in a noncompetitive retention election, as is done in other states.

These modifications, along with the defeats of 1972 and 1988, suggest the distrust Nevada's voters have of the "subterranean process of bar and bench politics in which there is little popular control" that is inherent in the merit selection process.[21] To control further the effects of "politics" in judicial selection, this section prohibits the state bar and the governor from appointing more than two members of the same party. Internal rules of the commission require that candidates be evaluated in "an impartial, objective manner" without considerations of "race, religion, sex or political affiliation of the applicant."[22]

This section has not been subject to interpretation.[23]

Sec: 21. Commission on judicial discipline

1. A justice of the supreme court or a district judge may, in addition to the provision of article 7 for impeachment, be censured, retired, or removed by the commission on judicial discipline. A justice or judge may appeal from the action of the commission to the supreme court, which may reverse such action or take any alternative action provided in this subsection.

2. The commission is composed of:

(a) Two justices or judges appointed by the supreme court;

(b) Two members of the State Bar of Nevada, a public corporation created by statute, appointed by its board of governors; and

(c) Three persons, not members of the legal profession, appointed by the governor.

The commission shall elect a chairman from among its three lay members.

3. If at any time the State Bar of Nevada ceases to exist as a public corporation or ceases to include all attorneys admitted to practice before the courts of this state, the legislature shall provide by law, or if it fails to do so the court shall provide by rule, for the appointment of attorneys at law to the positions designated in this section to be occupied by members of the State Bar of Nevada.

4. The term of office of each appointive member of the commission, except the first members, is 4 years. Each appointing authority shall appoint one of the members first appointed for a term of 2 years. If a vacancy occurs, the appointing authority shall fill the vacancy for the unexpired term. An appointing authority shall not appoint more than one resident of any county. The governor shall not appoint more than two members of the same political party. No member may be a member of a commission of judicial selection.

5. The supreme court shall make appropriate rules for:

(a) The confidentiality of all proceedings before the commission, except a decision to censure, retire or remove a justice or judge.

(b) The grounds of censure.

(c) The conduct of investigations and hearings.

6. No justice or judge may by virtue of this section be:

(a) Removed except for willful misconduct, willful or persistent failure to perform the duties of his office or habitual intemperance; or

(b) Retired except for advanced age which interferes with the proper performance of his judicial duties, or for mental or physical disability which prevents the proper performance of his judicial duties and which is likely to be permanent in nature.

7. Any person may bring to the attention of the commission any matter relating to the fitness of a justice or judge. The commission shall, after preliminary investigation, dismiss the matter or order a hearing to be held before it. If a hearing is ordered, a statement of the matter shall be served upon the justice or judge against whom the proceeding is brought. The commission in its discretion may suspend a justice or judge from the exercise of his office pending the determination of the proceedings before the commission. Any justice or judge whose removal is sought is liable to indictment and punishment according to law. A justice or judge retired for disability in accordance with this section is entitled thereafter to receive such compensation as the legislature may provide.

8. If a proceeding is brought against a justice of the supreme court, no justice may sit on the commission for that proceeding. If a proceeding is brought against a district judge, no judge from the same judicial district may sit on the commission for that proceeding. If an appeal is taken from an action of the commission to the supreme court, any justice who sat on the commission for that proceeding is disqualified from participating in the consideration or decision of the appeal. When any member of the commission is disqualified by this subsection, the supreme court shall appoint a substitute from among the eligible judges.

9. The commission may:

(a) Designate for each hearing an attorney or attorneys at law to act as counsel to conduct the proceeding;

(b) Summon witnesses to appear and testify under oath and compel the production of books, papers, documents and records;

(c) Grant immunity from prosecution or punishment when the commission deems it necessary and proper in order to compel the giving of testimony under oath and the production of books, papers, documents and records; and

(d) Exercise such further powers as the legislature may from time to time confer upon it.

Until the addition of section 21 in 1976, judges could only be removed by recall (Article 2, section 9), impeachment (Article 7, section 2), or legislative removal (Article 7, section 3). This section creates a special commission that exercises authority to censure, retire, or remove supreme court justices and district judges. In spite of the explicit failure of the language in this section to include judges of the justice and municipal courts, the attorney general has held that Article 7, section 4, authorizing the legislature to provide by law for the "removal from

Office of any Civil Officer . . . for Malfeasance or Nonfeasance,'' gives that body authority to include these judges within the provisions of this section, and they can be removed or retired, but not censured, by the Commission on Judicial Discipline (Attorney General's Opinion 81-4, March 3, 1981). Thus, although a district court judge or supreme court justice may be removed for ''willful misconduct, willful or persistent failure to perform the duties of his office or habitual intemperance'' and may be retired only for reasons of advanced age or mental or physical disability preventing the ''proper performance of his judicial duties,'' judges of the justice and municipal courts can be removed or retired only for reasons of malfeasance or nonfeasance.

Proceedings of the commission are confidential, but decisions to remove, retire, or censure a judge are not. No one may be a member of both the Commission on Judicial Selection and Commission on Judicial Discipline.

Article 7

Impeachment and Removal from Office

Sec: 1. **Impeachment: Trial; conviction**

> The Assembly shall have the sole power of impeaching. The concurrence of a majority of all the members elected, shall be necessary to an impeachment. All impeachments shall be tried by the Senate, and when sitting for that purpose, the Senators shall be upon Oath or Affirmation, to do justice according to Law and Evidence. The Chief Justice of the Supreme court [*sic*], shall preside over the Senate while sitting to try the Governor or Lieutenant Governor upon impeachment. No person shall be convicted without the concurrence of two thirds of the Senators elected.

The impeachment provisions of the Nevada Constitution are similar to those of the U.S. Constitution, with the lower house voting articles of impeachment by a simple majority vote and a trial in the upper house requiring a two-thirds majority for conviction and removal from office. The major difference between the two constitutions comes in the fact that federal impeachment and conviction is based on the appropriate majority of votes cast by those present, while state impeachment requires a majority of the assembly's total membership, and conviction demands a two-thirds vote of the total membership of the senate.

Given that the lieutenant governor serves as the presiding officer of the senate (Article 5, section 17), the convention delegates thought it inappropriate for that officer to preside over the impeachment trial of the governor since he or she would become acting governor upon the removal of the governor from office. In order to prevent that conflict of interest and the concomitant recriminations that would result should the governor be convicted, this section provides for the chief justice of the state supreme court to preside over the governor's impeachment trial.[24] That provision is similar to the U.S. Constitution's article on impeachment, which replaces the vice-president with the chief justice of the U.S. Supreme Court in the impeachment trial of the president (Article 1, section 3). Nevada also provides for the chief justice to preside over the impeachment trial of the lieutenant governor given that the president pro-tempore of the senate, who normally would preside, is next in the line of gubernatorial succession should the lieutenant governor be convicted (Article 5, section 17).

All constitutional, elective, and appointive state officers are impeachable under this article. The impeachment provisions are, thus, not limited to only "constitutional" or elective state officers (*Robison v. First Judicial District Court ex rel. County of Ormsby*).

Sec: 2. Officers subject to impeachment

> The Governor and other State and Judicial Officers, except Justices of the Peace shall be liable to impeachment for Misdemeanor or Malfeasance in Office; but judgment in such case shall not extend further than removal from Office and disqualification to hold any Office of honor, profit, or trust under this State. The party whether convicted or acquitted, shall, nevertheless, be liable to indictment, trial, judgment and punishment according to law.

This section provides a general definition of what constitutes an impeachable offense: misdemeanor or malfeasance in office. There has been no litigation on this issue, and the courts have not been required to define more specifically what might constitute such an offense. Section 2 also indicates that legislative punishment is limited to removal from office and disqualification for future office. This section clearly distinguishes an impeachment conviction from a criminal proceeding by explicitly noting that the former does not preclude the latter should the removed official have committed crimes while in office.

Justices of the peace are specifically excluded from removal by impeachment. The rationale behind this exclusion is not discussed in the debates of the convention but is most likely due to the minimal qualifications for the office and the fact that justice courts are not courts of record.

Sec: 3. Removal of supreme court justice or district judge

> For any reasonable cause to be entered on the journals of each House, which may, or may not be sufficient grounds for impeachment, the Chief Justice and Associate Justices of the Supreme Court and Judges of the District Courts shall be removed from Office on the vote of two thirds of the Members elected to each branch of the Legislature, and the Justice or Judge complained of, shall be served with a copy of the complaint against him, and shall have an opportunity of being heard in person or by counsel in his defense, Pro-

vided, that no member of either branch of the Legislature shall be eligible
to fill the vacancy occasioned by such removal.

This section provides a method, short of impeachment, whereby supreme court
justices and district court judges can be removed by the legislature. Although
the majority required is more stringent than that required for impeachment (a
two-thirds majority in both houses of the legislature), this procedure dispenses
with a formal impeachment hearing and trial and can be utilized quickly in an
emergency.

Legislative removal was hotly debated at the constitutional convention on the
grounds that it would interfere with the independence of the judiciary. However,
the combined fear of an incompetent judge who had not committed an impeachable offense remaining on the bench and the desire by the dominant mining
interests to have a less formal method than impeachment to remove "unfavorable
judicial opinion" led to its passage.[25]

This provision is exclusive and prohibits the use of other, less stringent means
to remove supreme court justices and district court judges legislatively (*State ex
rel. O'Neale v. McClinton*).

Sec: 4. **Removal of other civil officers**

Provision shall be made by law for the removal from Office of any Civil
Officer other than those in this Article previously specified, for Malfeasance,
or Nonfeasance in the Performance of his duties.

This section allows the legislature to provide for the removal of district, county,
township, and municipal officers short of the lengthy impeachment process. This
power is plenary, and so long as the statute is passed in the same manner as all
other laws and does not violate any other constitutional provisions, the legislature
may provide for special and summary removal proceedings; officers removed in
this way do not have a right to trial by jury (*Gay v. District Court of Tenth
Judicial District ex rel. Clark County; Bell v. First Judicial District Court*).

"Nonfeasance" has been defined by the courts as the "substantial failure to
perform a legal duty" (*Schumacher v. State ex rel. Furlong*).

Although justices of the peace and municipal court judges are not included in
the legislative removal provisions of section 3, the state attorney general has
upheld the state legislature's reliance on the plenary power granted in section 4
to give the Commission on Judicial Discipline the authority to remove and
involuntarily retire, but not censure, these courts of limited jurisdiction judges
(Attorney General's Opinion 81-4, March 3, 1981).

Municipal and Other Corporations

Sec: 1. **Corporations formed under general laws; municipal corporations formed under special acts**

> The Legislature shall pass no Special Act in any manner relating to corporate powers except Municipal purposes; but corporations may be formed under general laws; and all such laws may from time to time, be altered or repealed.

This section prohibits the legislature from passing special laws granting corporate powers. Historically, there had been substantial abuse by some state legislatures, often after having been bribed, to approve special laws favoring particular business corporations. The legislature is empowered by this section to provide general statutes such that corporations meeting the requirements are incorporated by the secretary of state.

This restriction on the legislature applies to "purely private corporations" (*In re Scott*) and prohibits the state from granting a corporation a right that could not be exercised by other corporations under the state's general incorporation laws (*State ex rel. Keith v. Dayton and Virginia Toll-Road Co.*).

The exception for "municipal purposes" allows the creation of municipalities by special acts (*State ex rel. Williams v. Second Judicial District Court ex rel. Churchill County*), as well as the general acts required under section 8. This exception has been read in its "broadest sense . . . to include public corporations" of all types, including nonpecuniary corporations such as the Nevada State Bar (*In re Scott*).

The prohibition in this section also applies to city governments, restricting them from adopting special laws relating to corporate powers not for municipal purposes (Attorney General's Opinion 89, November 12, 1963).

Sec: 2. **Corporate property subject to taxation; exemptions**

All real property, and possessory rights to the same, as well as personal property in this state, belonging to corporations now existing or hereafter created shall be subject to taxation, the same as property of individuals; Provided, that the property of corporations formed for Municipal, Charitable, Religious, or Educational purposes may be exempted by law.

This section has not been subject to significant interpretation but has been defined as meaning only "that the property of corporations shall be subject to the same taxation as the property of individuals" (*Sawyer v. Dooley*) and that such property also may include that outside the boundaries of the state but owned by a Nevada corporation (*State ex rel. United States Lines Co. v. Second Judicial District Court*).

Sec: 3. **Individual liability of corporators**

Dues from corporations shall be secured by such means as may be prescribed by law; Provided, that corporators in corporations formed under the laws of this State shall not be individually liable for the debts or liabilities of such corporation.

In order to promote capital investment within the state, section 3 protects investors by prohibiting "a member of the corporation, one of the stockholders or constituents of the body corporate" from being liable for a corporation's debts or liabilities (*Seaborn v. Wingfield*).

Sec: 4. **Regulation of corporations incorporated under territorial law**

Corporations created by or under the laws of the Territory of Nevada shall be subject to the provisions of such laws until the Legislature shall pass laws regulating the same, in pursuance of the provisions of this Constitution.

This was a transitional measure to govern territorial-created corporations until such time as the state legislature adopted state corporate laws. It is of historical interest only.

Sec: 5. **Corporations may sue and be sued**

Corporations may sue and be sued in all courts, in like manner as individuals.

Municipal corporations, including counties, are not exempt from suit by the U.S. Constitution's Eleventh Amendment; "they are liable for suits as individuals" under this section (*Lincoln County v. Luning*).

Sec: 6. **Circulation of certain bank notes or paper as money prohibited**

> No bank notes or paper of any kind shall ever be permitted to circulate as money in this State, except the Federal currency, and the notes of banks authorized under the laws of Congress.

The delegates at the 1864 convention were wary of and sought to prohibit the issuance of cheap paper money by state banks, often worthless currency that delegate George A. Nourse referred to as "infernal paper trash which has cursed almost every one of the Eastern States."[26] This section has not been subject to interpretation.

Sec: 7. **Eminent domain by corporations**

> No right of way shall be appropriated to the use of any corporation until full compensation be first made or secured therefor.

Article 1, section 8 provides constitutional authority for the state to condemn and take private property for a public use if it first provides just compensation to the owner. This section extends that power to the taking of such property for corporate use, again only with full compensation to the owner first. It has not been subject to interpretation.

Sec: 8. **Municipal corporations formed under general laws**

> The legislature shall provide for the organization of cities and towns by general laws and shall restrict their power of taxation, assessment, borrowing money, contracting debts and loaning their credit, except for procuring supplies of water; *provided, however*, that the legislature may, by general laws, in the manner and to the extent therein provided, permit and authorize the electors of any city or town to frame, adopt and amend a charter for its own government, or to amend any existing charter of such city or town.

Laws providing for the organization of cities and towns were not only left to the legislature but are, apparently, required by this section. In determining restrictions on their powers of taxation, assessment, borrowing money, contracting debts, and loaning credit, however, the legislature has plenary power and "alone has the power to determine the mode and measure of the restriction" (*State v.*

Rosenstock). When a state constitutional provision authorizes a municipality to act upon a particular matter, however, the legislature may not pass laws in conflict with it (*State ex rel. Owens v. Doxey*).

As noted in section 1, the state legislature may also pass special acts relating to municipal governments, as well as the general acts required in this section.

The water rights question had vehemently torn several of the western state constitutional conventions, but the Nevada delegates chose to leave the question of water rights to the legislature. In part, this was due to the fact that "Nevada statutory law already governed the use of water, and the schism of farmer-miner over water had not materially developed [in Nevada] by 1864."[27] Instead, the delegates debated only the issue of municipal indebtedness to procure water, deciding that various municipalities would require different amounts of indebtedness to procure sufficient water supplies and it would be unwise for the convention or the legislature to adopt what would, inevitably, be arbitrary restrictions.

The "home rule" provision of this section (beginning "provided however") was added by amendment in 1924, giving the legislature authority, which it has since exercised, to allow cities and towns to amend their charters without legislative approval (*Caton v. Frank*).

Sec: 9. **Gifts or loans of public money to certain corporations prohibited**

> The state shall not donate or loan money, or its credit, subscribe to or be, interested in the Stock of any company, association, or corporation, except corporations formed for educational and charitable purposes.

Article 8, section 9 of the 1863 constitution had allowed the state, with the approval of the people, to issue up to $3 million in bonds to build a railroad. That provision came under attack in the 1864 convention by those who thought the amount too small and by those who objected in principle to the state's loan of money to wealthy railroad corporations. The debate was both intense and long, with the final result being the rejection of a proposal similar to that in the 1863 constitution and a compromise proposal leaving the issue to the legislature with a bonding cap of $1.5 million. Primarily as a reaction to this railroad subsidy question, the convention adopted a total prohibition on such loans and donations to corporations. In 1992 the voters defeated by a three-to-one margin a proposed constitutional amendment to this section allowing the state to lend its money or credit to corporations and to own stock in corporations.

The provisions of this section have been interpreted to apply only to municipal and other corporations; it does not prohibit loans to individuals (Attorney General's Opinion 35, March 28, 1919).

The restrictions enacted by this section do not prohibit the investment of funds contributed in trust, such as public employees' retirement funds, since these funds cannot be repossessed by the legislature for other uses (Attorney General's Opinion 35, April 6, 1959). Article 9, section 2, as amended in 1974, segregated these retirement funds and specifically prohibited the legislature from using them for any other purpose.

Sec: 10. Loans of public money to or ownership of stock in certain corporations by county or municipal corporations prohibited

> No county, city, town, or other municipal corporation shall become a stockholder in any joint stock company, corporation or association whatever, or- loan its credit in aid of any such company, corporation or association, except, railroad corporations, companies or associations.

This section applies the restrictions of section 9 to counties and municipalities, with two important exceptions. First, unlike the state, these entities are allowed to loan their credit to or own stock in railroad companies. Second, although section 9 prohibits the donation of any state money to corporations, section 10 does not include a similar provision restricting counties and municipalities. Thus, in view of the lack of an express prohibition in the constitution, the state legislature may authorize counties and municipalities to donate money to any company (*Gibson v. Mason*).

Bonds for which the county or city are not liable, such as housing bonds and economic development bonds payable only out of the funds of these authorities and not general municipal revenues, do not violate this section (*McLaughlin v. Housing Authority; State ex rel. Brennan v. Bowman*).

Article 9

Finance and State Debt

Sec: 1. **Fiscal year**

The fiscal year shall commence on the first day of July of each year.

As originally enacted, section 1 began the fiscal year on January 1 but was amended in 1930 to begin July 1. Since the legislative session opens in January, this very practical change gives that body six months to enact a budget prior to the start of the fiscal year.

Sec: 2. **Annual tax for state expenses; trust funds for compensation for industrial accidents, occupational diseases and public employees' retirement system**

The legislature shall provide by law for an annual tax sufficient to defray the estimated expenses of the state for each fiscal year; and whenever the expenses of any year shall exceed the income, the legislature shall provide for levying a tax sufficient, with other sources of income, to pay the deficiency, as well as the estimated expenses of such ensuing year or two years. Any moneys paid for the purpose of providing compensation for industrial accidents and occupational diseases, and for administrative expenses incidental thereto, and for the purpose of funding and administering a public employees' retirement system, shall be segregated in proper accounts in the state treasury, and such moneys shall never be used for any other purposes, and they are hereby declared to be trust funds for the uses and purposes herein specified.

Unlike Congress, the Nevada legislature, like those in other states, is required
to balance its budget. Because the legislature meets biennially, it is in the
unenviable position of having to develop revenue and spending projections for
a two-year period. Sometimes, as in the 1991–1993 biennium, these figures are
wrong. This section would seem to require that the legislature meet for the
purpose of increasing revenues to meet any such shortfall. In such circumstances,
however, the governor, as chief executive, makes cuts in the agencies under his
authority to ensure a balanced budget.

Amendments to this section in 1956 and 1974 declared that Nevada Industrial
Commission and Public Employee Retirement System funds, respectively, were
trust funds and could not be reappropriated by the legislature for any other
purposes.

Section 2 has not been subject to significant interpretation.

Sec: 3. **State indebtedness: Limitations and exceptions**

The state may contract public debts; but such debts shall never, in the
aggregate, exclusive of interest, exceed the sum of two per cent of the
assessed valuation of the state, as shown by the reports of the county assessors
to the state controller, except for the purpose of defraying extraordinary
expenses, as hereinafter mentioned. Every such debt shall be authorized by
law for some purpose or purposes, to be distinctly specified therein; and
every such law shall provide for levying an annual tax sufficient to pay the
interest semiannually, and the principal within twenty years from the passage
of such law, and shall specially appropriate the proceeds of said taxes to
the payment of said principal and interest; and such appropriation shall not
be repealed nor the taxes postponed or diminished until the principal and
interest of said debts shall have been wholly paid. Every contract of indebtedness entered into or assumed by or on behalf of the state, when all
its debts and liabilities amount to said sum before mentioned, shall be void
and of no effect, except in cases of money borrowed to repel invasion,
suppress insurrection, defend the state in time of war, or, if hostilities be
threatened, provide for the public defense.

The state, notwithstanding the foregoing limitations, may, pursuant to
authority of the legislature, make and enter into any and all contracts necessary, expedient or advisable for the protection and preservation of any of
its property or natural resources, or for the purposes of obtaining the benefits
thereof, however arising and whether arising by or through any undertaking
or project of the United States or by or through the treaty or compact between
the states, or otherwise. The legislature may from time to time make such
appropriations as may be necessary to carry out the obligations of the state
under such contracts, and shall levy such tax as may be necessary to pay
the same or carry them into effect.

The bonding authority authorized by this section was provided "to enable the
state to maintain its business upon a cash basis, notwithstanding financial exi-

gencies, without resorting to onerous taxation" (*Klein v. Kinkead*). As originally enacted, section 3 placed a $300,000 cap on the state's bonding capacity. The inadvisability of establishing a specific cap was not debated in the convention; however, over time, the state began to have difficulty making capital improvements because these often had to be paid for out of current revenues. In response, this section was amended in 1916 to 1 percent of the state's assessed valuation and, after a defeat by the voters in 1960, to 2 percent in 1989.

Whether a bond is considered a debt under this section does not depend on the type of tax imposed to fund it. Bonds funded by ad valorem or excise taxes are considered to fall within the limitations of this provision. However, bonds funded by user fees or other nontax revenues ("special funds") are not included within the 2 percent limitation of this section (*Morris v. Board of Regents of the University of Nevada*). More generally, any bonds that are not secured by the "public faith and credit of the state" are not considered "debts" under section 3 (Attorney General's Opinion 13, March 5, 1963).

So as not to tie the hands of the legislature too severely, section 3 allows two exceptions to the bonding cap. The last sentence of the first paragraph was added at the urging of several convention delegates to ensure that the state would not be handicapped in its ability to respond to a hostile crisis even though it might have reached its bonding cap.

The importance to the convention's delegates of natural resource development in Nevada is evident in the second paragraph, which excludes bonds for the preservation of the state's property and natural resources from the definition of debt. The exemption applies to "all natural resources found within the geographical limits of Nevada," including water. Furthermore, the legislature, in acting in this regard, is broadly exempted from "all the limitations formed in the first paragraph," including the "amount of debt, the term for which it may be contracted, and the requirement of a specific tax appropriated for its repayment" (*State ex rel. State General Obligation Bond Commission v. Koontz*). However, a scheme whereby the state pays an annual fee to a landowner for a certain period of time, after which the land reverts to the state, does not fall within this natural resources exception (Attorney General's Opinion 3, January 29, 1959).

Sec: 4. **Assumption of debts of county, city or corporation by state**

The State shall never assume the debts of any county, town, city or other corporation whatever, unless such debts have been created to repel invasion, suppress insurrection or to provide for the public defense.

This section has not been subject to significant interpretation.

Sec: 5. Proceeds from fees for licensing and registration of motor vehicles and excise taxes on fuel reserved for construction, maintenance and repair of public highways; exception

The proceeds from the imposition of any license or registration fee and other charge with respect to the operation of any motor vehicle upon any public highway in this state and the proceeds from the imposition of any excise tax on gasoline or other motor vehicle fuel shall, except costs of administration, be used exclusively for the construction, maintenance, and repair of the public highways of this state. The provisions of this section do not apply to the proceeds of any tax imposed upon motor vehicles by the legislature in lieu of an ad valorem property tax.

Section 5 was added in 1940 in order to earmark fuel taxes and motor licenses and fees for the specific purpose of construction, maintenance, and repair of public highways. This not only ensures that highway users will pay the costs of these facilities but also that the legislature cannot reappropriate the funds to nonhighway uses.

The restrictions on the use of Highway Fund moneys have been strictly adhered to by the state. These funds can be used for county roads (Attorney General's Opinion 417, January 29, 1947) but not to build airports (Attorney General's Opinion 891, March 10, 1950) or to purchase traffic enforcement vehicles (Attorney General's Opinion 6, January 15, 1951) since these do not constitute construction, maintenance, or repair of public highways. However, "construction" has been broadly defined to include not only the physical aspects of grading and paving roads but to "everything connected with and necessarily incidental to the complete accomplishment" of highway construction, including payment to private utility companies for the relocation of facilities located on or in highways (Attorney General's Opinion 86, November 7, 1963).

The last sentence was added by constitutional amendment in 1962 to exempt from these restrictions any motor vehicle fees adopted by the legislature in lieu of an ad valorem property tax. As noted under Article 10, section 1, that section of the constitution was also amended in 1962, authorizing the legislature to adopt such fees in lieu of property taxes on automobiles as a result of an attorney general's opinion that the latter fell within the constraints of Article 10's requirement that personal property taxes, even those on motor vehicles, be at a "uniform and equal rate" (Attorney General's Opinion 68, June 29, 1959).

Article 10

Taxation

Sec: 1. Uniform and equal rate of assessment and taxation; exceptions and exemptions; inheritance and income taxes prohibited

1. The legislature shall provide by law for a uniform and equal rate of assessment and taxation, and shall prescribe such regulations as shall secure a just valuation for taxation of all property, real, personal and possessory, except mines and mining claims, which shall be assessed and taxed only as provided in section 5 of this article.

2. Shares of stock, bonds, mortgages, notes, bank deposits, book accounts and credits, and securities and choses in action of like character are deemed to represent interest in property already assessed and taxed, either in Nevada or elsewhere, and shall be exempt.

3. The legislature may constitute agricultural and open-space real property having a greater value for another use than that for which it is being used, as a separate class for taxation purposes and may provide a separate uniform plan for appraisal and valuation of such property for assessment purposes. If such plan is provided, the legislature shall also provide for retroactive assessment for a period of not less than 7 years when agricultural and open-space real property is converted to a higher use conforming to the use for which other nearby property is used.

4. Personal property which is moving in interstate commerce through or over the territory of the State of Nevada, or which was consigned to a warehouse, public or private, within the State of Nevada from outside the State of Nevada for storage in transit to a final destination outside the State of Nevada, whether specified when transportation begins or afterward, shall be deemed to have acquired no situs in Nevada for purposes of taxation and

shall be exempt from taxation. Such property shall not be deprived of such exemption because while in the warehouse the property is assembled, bound, joined, processed, disassembled, divided, cut, broken in bulk, relabeled or repackaged.

5. The legislature may exempt motor vehicles from the provisions of the tax required by this section, and in lieu thereof, if such exemption is granted, shall provide for a uniform and equal rate of assessment and taxation of motor vehicles, which rate shall not exceed five cents on one dollar of assessed valuation.

6. The legislature shall provide by law for a progressive reduction in the tax upon business inventories by 20 percent in each year following the adoption of this provision, and after the expiration of the 4th year such inventories are exempt from taxation. The legislature may exempt any other personal property, including livestock.

7. No inheritance tax shall ever be levied.

8. The legislature may exempt by law property used for municipal, educational, literary, scientific or other charitable purposes, or to encourage the conservation of energy or the substitution of other sources for fossil sources of energy.

9. No income tax shall be levied upon the wages or personal income of natural persons. Notwithstanding the foregoing provision, and except as otherwise provided in subsection 1 of this section, taxes may be levied upon the income or revenue of any business in whatever form it may be conducted for profit in the state.

Although many sections of the constitution are broadly written, the taxation article tends to "constitutionalize" various tax provisions that probably should have been left to the legislature. It is, perhaps, not surprising that section 1, representing attempts to protect from the legislature various political interests at a particular time of dominance, has been amended twelve times since 1864 in response to changing political circumstances.

A clear principle drawn from the legal interpretation of this section by the courts and the attorney general is that taxation should be "uniform and equal" and that "one species of taxable property should not pay a higher rate of taxes than other kinds of property" (*State v. Eastabrook*; Attorney General's Opinion 59, May 29, 1913). The one exception, not surprisingly, is mines and mining claims (see section 5). Although ad valorem taxes must be uniform, the manner of assessing and collecting these taxes is not required to be uniform (*Sawyer v. Dooley*). It does not violate this section for the legislature to provide a property tax exemption for veterans (*Hendel v. Weaver*), nor is it a violation that the costs of professional and business licenses vary (*Ex parte Robinson*).

Paragraph 4 was added in 1960 to establish Nevada as a free port. Property moving through the state in interstate commerce "acquires no situs . . . for purposes of taxation and is exempt from all forms of taxation, including property tax and excise tax'' (Attorney General's Opinion 79-16, July 24, 1979). Licensing and tax requirements do not apply until the property ''is reconsigned to destination within [the] state'' (Attorney General's Opinion 79-16, July 24, 1979).

Paragraph 5 was added in 1962 as a response to a 1959 attorney general's opinion holding that the personal property tax on motor vehicles was an ad valorem tax and was subject to the paragraph 1 provision requiring a ''uniform and equal rate of assessment and taxation'' (Attorney General's Opinion 68, June 29, 1959). This paragraph allows the legislature to establish a uniform motor vehicle tax in lieu of personal property taxes on such vehicles.

The prohibition on inheritance and estate taxes was added in 1942 but is limited by section 4, added in 1986.

Paragraph 6, allowing for an exemption of property used for municipal, educational, literary, scientific, or other charitable purposes, was included in the original 1864 constitution and has been held to include the YMCA (Attorney General's Opinion 264, October 11, 1965) and water mains and other municipal water supply system equipment located outside city limits (Attorney General's Opinion 353, August 29, 1946) but not to a ranch owned but not operated by the city (Attorney General's Opinion 353, August 29, 1946) or a nonprofit rural electrification cooperative corporation organized for the purpose of receiving federal loans (Attorney General's Opinion 12, February 20, 1959). The language allowing for exemption for energy conservation or fossil fuel alternatives was added in 1982 in response to the energy crisis of the 1970s. It has not been subject to legal interpretation.

Personal income taxes had long been prohibited by state statute, but concern over the possibility of legislative reversal led to a successful 1988 and 1990 initiative to add paragraph 9 to this section ''constitutionalizing'' that prohibition and putting it outside the reach of the legislature. It does, however, allow for a tax on the income or revenue of for-profit businesses in the state.

Sec: 2. **Total tax levy for public purposes limited**

> The total tax levy for all public purposes including levies for bonds, within
> the state, or any subdivision thereof, shall not exceed five cents on one
> dollar of assessed valuation.

This section was added by constitutional amendment in 1936. The tax levy limitation has been held to apply to a tax levied for support of a fire protection district ''because such tax is for a public purpose and not for a special or local benefit'' (Attorney General's Opinion 262, October 4, 1965). For the same reason, it is applicable to a tax for groundwater basin administration imposed on all taxable property in the basin but not to a special assessment on water users (Attorney General's Opinion 125, April 20, 1973). The limitation has been held not to apply to other special use taxes, such as sewer use charges (*Harris v. City of Reno*), or a tax on livestock to support the stock inspection fund (Attorney General's Opinion 69, July 9, 1959).

Sec: 3. **Household goods and furniture of single household exempt**

> All household goods and furniture used by a single household and owned by a member of that household are exempt from taxation.

Section 3 was added by initiative in the elections of 1980 and 1982 and has not been subject to interpretation.

Sec: 3[A]. **Food exempt from taxes on retail sales; exceptions**

> The legislature shall provide by law for:
>
> 1. The exemption of food for human consumption from any tax upon the sale, storage, use or consumption of tangible personal property; and
>
> 2. These commodities to be excluded from any such exemption:
>
> (a) Prepared food intended for immediate consumption.
>
> (b) Alcoholic beverages.

The sales tax exemption on food, added in 1984, has not been subject to interpretation.

Sec: 4. **Taxation of estates taxed by United States; limitations**

> The legislature may provide by law for the taxation of estates taxed by the United States, but only to the extent of any credit allowed by federal law for the payment of the state tax and only for the purpose of education, to be divided between the common schools and the state university for their support and maintenance. The combined amount of these federal and state taxes may not exceed the estate tax which would be imposed by federal law alone. If another state of the United States imposes and collects death taxes against an estate which is taxable by the State of Nevada under this section, the amount of estate tax to be collected by the State of Nevada must be reduced by the amount of the death taxes collected by the other state. Any lien for the estate tax attaches no sooner than the time when the tax is due and payable, and no restriction on possession or use of a decedent's property may be imposed by law before the time when the tax is due and payable in full under federal law. The State of Nevada shall:
>
> 1. Accept the determination by the United States of the amount of the taxable estate without further audit.

2. Accept payment of the tax in installments proportionate to any which may be permitted under federal law.

3. Impose no penalty for such a deferred payment.

4. Not charge interest on a deferred or belated payment at any rate higher than may be provided in similar circumstances by federal law.

Prior to the addition of section 4 in 1986, Nevada had been unable, as a result of section 1 of this article, to pick up its share of the federal estate tax credit. Nevada was the only state not to do so, but the voters, fearing additional taxes, defeated this amendment in 1982. With assurances that this section would not create any new or increased taxes, the voters approved it in 1986, allowing the state to reap millions of dollars on the estates of wealthy individuals, many of whom had taken up residence in Nevada because of its lack of a personal income tax and generally low tax rates. This section has not been subject to interpretation.

Sec: 5. Tax on proceeds of minerals; appropriation to counties; apportionment; assessment and taxation of mines

1. The legislature shall provide by law for a tax upon the net proceeds of all minerals, including oil, gas and other hydrocarbons, extracted in this state, at a rate not to exceed 5 percent of the net proceeds. No other tax may be imposed upon a mineral or its proceeds until the identity of the proceeds as such is lost.

2. The legislature shall appropriate to each county that sum which would be produced by levying a tax upon the entire amount of the net proceeds taxed in each taxing district in the county at the rate levied in the district upon the assessed valuation of real property. The total amount so appropriated to each county must be apportioned among the respective governmental units and districts within it, including the county itself and the school district, in the same proportion as they share in the total taxes collected on property according to value.

3. Each patented mine or mining claim must be assessed and taxed as other real property is assessed and taxed, except that no value may be attributed to any mineral known or believed to underlie it, and no value may be attributed to the surface of a mine or claim if one hundred dollars' worth of labor has been actually performed on the mine or claim during the year preceding the assessment.

Mining taxation was hotly debated in both the 1863 and 1864 conventions and was responsible, in part, for the defeat of the 1863 document. The mining taxation provisions have been amended a number of times over the years, with the current situation reflected in section 5, which was added in a special election in 1989.

This section allows for the taxation of minerals, including oil and gas, at a rate different from other property (see section 1) and limits other taxes (e.g., severance taxes) that can be imposed on minerals and their proceeds.

Paragraph 3, carried over from a 1906 amendment to section 1, is designed to encourage individuals and corporations to prospect mining claims rather than allow them to lie dormant. Thus, a mining claim in which one-hundred dollars' worth of labor has been performed will be taxed only on its net proceeds, while those lying dormant will be assessed and taxed the same as other real property (*Goldfield Consolidated Company v. State*). In the case of a dormant mining claim, however, taxes must be assessed based on the surface value, not on the value of minerals underlying it.

Article 11

Education

Sec: 1. **Legislature to encourage education; appointment, term and duties of superintendent of public instruction**

> The legislature shall encourage by all suitable means the promotion of intellectual, literary, scientific, mining, mechanical, agricultural, and moral improvements, and also provide for a superintendent of public instruction and by law prescribe the manner of appointment, term of office and the duties thereof.

As originally enacted, this section made the superintendent of public instruction an elective office. An amendment in 1956 made the office appointive; by statute, the superintendent is appointed by the popularly elected state board of education. This section has not been subject to significant interpretation.

Sec: 2. **Uniform system of common schools**

> The legislature shall provide for a uniform system of common schools, by which a school shall be established and maintained in each school district at least six months in every year, and any school district which shall allow instruction of a sectarian character therein may be deprived of its proportion of the interest of the public school fund during such neglect or infraction, and the legislature may pass such laws as will tend to secure a general attendance of the children in each school district upon said public schools.

This section contains the first of three separate, and increasingly severe, prohibitions in Article 11 on sectarian instruction. It prohibits common schools that engage in sectarian instruction from receiving moneys from the public school fund. "Common schools" and "public schools" are synonymous and are defined as those "supported by taxation, open to all of suitable age and attainments, free of expense, and under the control of agents appointed by the voters" (Attorney General's Opinion 89, August 6, 1951); sectarian schools are not considered common or public schools (Attorney General's Opinion, September 2, 1909).

Although school facilities may be rented to religious groups to present exhibitions or shows, open to the general public, that do not attempt to impart religious teachings (Attorney General's Opinion 14, February 23, 1955), these facilities cannot be used by religious groups for "sectarian purposes" (Attorney General's Opinion 316, February 19, 1954; Attorney General's Opinion 14, February 23, 1955). Neither of the latter opinions has been challenged in the courts since congressional passage of a statute guaranteeing equal access to school facilities.

If federal grant moneys are kept separate from the public school fund noted in this section, it is not a violation for a school district to provide, as required by the federal grant, aid to educationally deprived students in private schools (Attorney General's Opinion 276, November 5, 1965).

Sec: 3. Pledge of certain property and money, escheated estates and fines collected under penal laws for educational purposes; apportionment and use of interest

> All lands granted by Congress to this state for educational purposes, all estates that escheat to the state, all property given or bequeathed to the state for educational purposes, and the proceeds derived from these sources, together with that percentage of the proceeds from the sale of federal lands which has been granted by Congress to this state without restriction or for educational purposes and all fines collected under the penal laws of the state are hereby pledged for educational purposes and the money therefrom must not be transferred to other funds for other uses. The interest only earned on the money derived from these sources must be apportioned by the legislature among the several counties for educational purposes, and, if necessary, a portion of that interest may be appropriated for the support of the state university, but any of that interest which is unexpended at the end of any year must be added to the principal sum pledged for educational purposes.

The "lands granted by Congress" in this section refer to the 90,000 acres that Nevada received upon becoming a state as a result of the Morrill Act of 1862. Money derived from the sale of public lands, all estates escheated to the state, property given to the state for education, and fines collected by the state are deposited into the State Permanent School Fund. The interest derived from this fund is placed in the State Distributive School Fund and apportioned to the counties for educational purposes only, with the proviso that some of this interest may be given to the state university.

Funds derived from the sale of these pledged lands cannot be used for anything other than educational purposes (*Heydenfeldt v. Daney Gold & Silver Mining Co.*), a restriction that applies to both principal and interest (*State ex rel. Keith v. Westerfield*).

Fines collected under the state's penal laws include fines from military courts (Attorney General's Opinion 172, June 6, 1935), fines collected in justice court for state violations (Attorney General's Opinion 150, February 28, 1950), and fines collected under county penal laws (Attorney General's Opinion 303, November 17, 1953) but not fines for violations of city ordinances (*State v. Rosenstock*), forfeitures (Attorney General's Opinion 167, February 10, 1925), or forfeitures of bail (Attorney General's Opinion 16, March 20, 1963).

Sec: 4. **Establishment of state university; control by board of regents**

> The Legislature shall provide for the establishment of a State University which shall embrace departments for Agriculture, Mechanic Arts, and Mining to be controlled by a Board of Regents whose duties shall be prescribed by Law.

The specific inclusion of agriculture and mechanic arts in this section is designed to allow the state to take advantage of the Morrill Act, which granted seventy-two sections of land to Nevada to support creation of a land-grant college.

The elected board of regents possesses "exclusive executive and administrative control of the university" (*King v. Board of Regents*), but its judicial or quasi-judicial acts are reviewable by the courts (*State ex rel. Richardson v. Board of Regents*). Community colleges established by the state are also administered by the board of regents, and the legislature is prohibited by this section from creating a separate body for that purpose (Attorney General's Opinion 479, January 10, 1968).

The University and Community College System of Nevada is a "constitutional corporation" independent of the other branches of government. Thus, although Article 3's separation of powers provision prohibits a state employee from serving in the state legislature (Attorney General's Opinion 357, December 12, 1954), this rule has not been applied to university or community college professors.

Sec: 5. **Establishment of normal schools and grades of schools; oath of teachers and professors**

> The Legislature shall have power to establis [*sic*] Normal schools, and such different grades of schools, from the primary department to the University, as in their discretion they may deem necessary, and all Professors in said University, or Teachers in said Schools of whatever grade, shall be required to take and subscribe to the oath as prescribed in Article Fifteenth of this

Constitution. No Professor or Teacher who fails to comply with the provisions of any law framed in accordance with the provisions of this Section,
shall be entitled to receive any portion of the public monies set apart for
school purposes.

This section gives the legislature authority to establish "any educational program
it deems necessary up to the college level," including vocational, technical, and
adult education programs (Attorney General's Opinion 146, June 8, 1964). It
has not been subject to judicial interpretation.

Sec: 6. **Support of university and common schools by direct legislative appropriation**

In addition to other means provided for the support and maintenance of said
university and common schools, the legislature shall provide for their support
and maintenance by direct legislative appropriation from the general fund,
upon the presentation of budgets in the manner required by law.

This section provides for additional educational funds from the state's general
fund above and beyond those outlined in section 3. However, any funds generated
by the university through grants and similar sources over and above that estimated
by the legislature must, by legislative statute, be returned to the general fund
(Attorney General's Opinion 80-7, March 18, 1980).

Given that the university system is a branch of the state government and any
judgments against it would have to paid from the general fund, the university
and the board of regents are immune from suit for monetary damages by virtue
of the Eleventh Amendment to the U.S. Constitution (*Johnson v. University of
Nevada*). Entities created by the board of regents, such as a campus police force,
are similarly immune from such suits (*Meza v. Lee*).

Sec: 7. **Board of regents: Election and duties**

The Governor, Secretary of State, and Superintendent of Public Instruction,
shall for the first Four Years and until their successors are elected and
qualified constitute a Board of Regents to control and manage the affairs of
the University and the funds of the same under such regulations as may be
provided by law. But the Legislature shall at its regular session next preceding
the expiration of the term of Office of said Board of Regents provide for
the election of a new Board of Regents and define their duties.

Members of the board of regents must be elected by the people; vacancies between
elections must, under the requirements of Article 17, section 22, be filled by
the governor and not by the legislature (*State ex rel. Dickerson v. Elwell*). The

legislature may, however, establish terms of office for the board of regents (*Tam v. Colton*).

The legislature may establish statutory powers and duties of the board of regents (Attorney General's Opinion 881, February 18, 1950) but may not infringe on the powers vested in the board by this section (Attorney General's Opinion 290, July 23, 1957). Although the board has authority to manage and control the affairs of the university, the legislature may also establish "reasonable safeguards" over the expenditure of state funds appropriated to the university (Attorney General's Opinion 146, March 21, 1960) and may attach conditions to the expenditure of appropriated moneys (Attorney General's Opinion 124, April 14, 1964).

Sec: 8. Immediate organization and maintenance of state university

The Board of Regents shall, from the interest accruing from the first funds which come under their control, immediately organize and maintain the said Mining department in such manner as to make it most effective and useful, Provided, that all the proceeds of the public lands donated by Act of Congress approved July second A.D. Eighteen hundred and sixty two, for a college for the benefit of Agriculture, the Mechanics Arts, and including Military tactics shall be invested by the said Board of Regents in a separate fund to be appropriated exclusively for the benefit of the first named departments to the University as set forth in Section Four above; And the Legislature shall provide that if through neglect or any other contingency, any portion of the fund so set apart, shall be lost or misappropriated, the State of Nevada shall replace said amount so lost or misappropriated in said fund so that the principal of said fund shall remain forever undiminished.

This section, along with section 4, indicates the importance of mining to the drafters of the constitution. It has not been subject to significant interpretation.

Sec: 9. Sectarian instruction prohibited in common schools and university

No sectarian instruction shall be imparted or tolerated in any school or University that may be established under this Constitution.

Section 9 goes beyond the sectarian instruction provision in section 2 by prohibiting such instruction outright (section 2 merely deprives schools that do so of public school funds). Section 9 also applies this restriction to the university, as well as the common schools included in section 2.

The prohibition included here, generally interpreted in a parallel manner to the First Amendment establishment clause, applies not only to state-funded sectarian instruction but also to volunteers seeking to engage in religious instruction on school property before, during, or after school hours (Attorney General's Opinion 684, October 4, 1948).

Sec: 10. **No public money to be used for sectarian purposes**

> No public funds of any kind or character whatever, State, County or Municipal, shall be used for sectarian purpose.

Section 10, added by constitutional amendment in 1880, goes beyond the proscriptions of sections 2 and 9 by prohibiting the use of public funds, "directly or indirectly, for the building up of any sect" (*State ex rel. Nevada Orphan Asylum v. Hallock*). The plain words of this prohibition appear to apply to all uses of public funds and not solely educational programs, although most of the litigation in this area has involved education spending. Thus, whereas the constitution's Ordinance and Article 1, section 4 provide for protection of the free exercise of religion, this provision prohibits the establishment of religion in the state. Consequently, long before the U.S. Supreme Court applied the religion clauses of the Bill of Rights to the states in *Cantwell v. Connecticut* and *Everson v. Board of Education*, both rights were guaranteed under the state constitution.

The state may use its funds to hospitalize crippled children in a sectarian hospital where no instruction is given (Attorney General's Opinion B-40, February 11, 1941), but it may not use public funds to teach parochial students who are ill and at home (Attorney General's Opinion 209, September 12, 1956) or to teach parochial students in public school classes that are unavailable to them at their parochial schools (Attorney General's Opinion 278, November 15, 1965).

This section prohibits the state from giving state employees leave with pay to attend religious services (Attorney General's Opinion 79-A, April 12, 1979) but does not prevent the payment of chaplains at state prisons for performing noncompulsory religious services (Attorney General's Opinion 67, September 5, 1963).

Article 12

Militia

Sec: 1. **Legislature to provide for militia**

The Legislature shall provide by law for organizing and disciplining the Militia of this State, for the effectual encouragement of Volunteer Corps and the safe keeping of the public Arms.

Sec: 2. **Power of governor to call out militia**

The Governor shall have power to call out the Militia to execute the laws of the State or to suppress insurrection or repel invasion.

Following the federal lead, Nevada provides for civilian control over the military (see Article 1, section 11) by making the legislature responsible for the organization of the state militia, with the governor acting as commander in chief (see Article 5, section 5). Article 12 has not been subject to any significant legal interpretation.

Article 13

Public Institutions

Sec: 1. Institutions for insane, blind, deaf and dumb to be fostered and supported by state

> Institutions for the benefit of the Insane, Blind and Deaf and Dumb, and such other benevolent institutions as the public good may require, shall be fostered and supported by the State, subject to such regulations as may be prescribed by law.

This section has not been subject to any significant legal interpretation.

Sec: 2. State prison: Establishment and maintenance; juvenile offenders

> A State Prison shall be established and maintained in such manner as may be prescribed by law, and provision may be made by law for the establishment and maintainance [*sic*] of a House of Refuge for Juvenile Offenders.

The creation and maintenance of a state prison system is left to the legislature, which has established a Department of Prisons headed by a gubernatorially appointed director. Article 5, section 21 establishes the Board of State Prison Commissioners (governor, secretary of state, attorney general) to supervise the state prison system.

Sec: 3. **County public welfare**

[Repealed in 1937.]

Prior to its repeal, this section provided, ''The respective counties of the State shall provide as may be prescribed by law, for those inhabitants who, by reason of age and infirmity or misfortunes, may have claim upon the sympathy and aid of Society.'' The state supreme court had relied on this provision to strike down an attempt by the legislature to establish a state asylum for paupers (*State ex rel. Keyser v. Hallock*); its repeal was necessary in order for the state to participate in New Deal–era federal old-age assistance programs.

Article 14

Boundary

Sec: 1. **Boundary of the state of Nevada**

The boundary of the State of Nevada is as follows: Commencing at a point formed by the intersection of the forty-third degree of longitude West from Washington with the forty-second degree of North latitude; thence due East along the forty-second degree of North latitude to its intersection with the thirty-seventh degree of longitude West from Washington; thence South on the thirty-seventh degree of longitude West from Washington to its intersection with the middle line of the Colorado River of the West; thence down the middle line of the Colorado River of the West to its intersection with the Eastern boundary of the State of California; thence in a North Westerly direction along the Eastern boundary line of the State of California to the forty-third degree of Longitude West from Washington; Thence North along the forty-third degree of West Longitude, and the Eastern boundary line of the State of California to the place of beginning. All territory lying West of and adjoining the boundary line herein prescribed, which the State of California may relinquish to the Territory or State of Nevada, shall thereupon be embraced within and constitute a part of this state.

In 1866 Congress gave Nevada additional territory, which had not been included in the original 1864 boundary. The state legislature accepted the addition in 1867 but failed to amend the constitution to reflect that fact. In 1982, this section was finally amended to reflect the actual boundary of the state as it has existed since 1867, including one degree farther east, Clark County, lower Nye County, the tip of Esmeralda County, and a strip of Lincoln County.

Article 15

Miscellaneous Provisions

Sec: 1. **Carson City seat of government**

> The seat of Government shall be at Carson City, but no appropriation for the erection or purchase of Capitol buildings shall be made during the next three Years.

Territorial Governor Nye mandated that the first territorial legislature meet in Carson City in 1861. The legislature designated Carson City as the capital at that time, and the 1864 constitution reaffirmed that decision, although some delegates had wanted to leave this designation to the first state legislature. This section has not been subject to legal interpretation.

Sec: 2. **Oath of office**

> Members of the legislature, and all officers, executive, judicial and ministerial, shall, before they enter upon the duties of their respective offices, take and subscribe to the following oath:

> I, _____, do solemly [*sic*] swear (or affirm) that I will support, protect and defend the constitution and government of the United States, and the constitution and government of the State of Nevada, against all enemies, whether domestic or foreign, and that I will bear true faith, allegiance and loyalty to the same, any ordinance, resolution or law of any state notwithstanding, and that I will well and faithfully perform all the duties of the office of _____, on which I am about to enter; (if an oath) so help me God; (if an affirmation) under the pains and penalties of perjury.

This section was amended in 1914 to eliminate a lengthy portion of the oath in which the oath takers had to swear that they had not taken part in any duel since the adoption of the state's constitution and that they would not do so while in office. Employees who are not required to take the oath mandated by this section are not considered *officers* under the state constitution (*State ex rel. Kendall v. Cole*).

Sec: 3. **Eligibility for public office**

> No person shall be eligible to any office who is not a qualified elector under this constitution.

The courts and attorney general have been quite liberal in interpreting who may run for office. Qualifications for being an elector are established in Article 2, section 1.

The right to hold office is "one of the valuable rights of citizenship," and any ambiguities in the law should be "resolved in favor of eligibility to office" (*Gilbert v. Breithaupt*).

Unless constitutionally or statutorily required, a candidate for office need not be a resident of the district he or she is seeking to represent: "The right of the people to select from citizens and qualified electors whomsoever they please to fill an elective office is not to be circumscribed except by legal provisions clearly limiting the right" (*State ex rel. Schur v. Payne*).

It is not necessary that one be a registered voter to hold office. Registration is not a qualification of an elector but a "mere condition to the right to vote" (Attorney General's Opinion 68, March 30, 1916; Attorney General's Opinion 327, July 19, 1946). The right to hold office has been held not to be coextensive with the right to vote (Attorney General's Opinion 186, July 11, 1956). It is not a violation of this section for a political party to require a primary candidate to be a registered voter of the party for which he or she is seeking the nomination; however, candidates in nonpartisan primaries cannot be required to be registered voters (Attorney General's Opinion 197, January 27, 1976).

Qualified electors between the ages of eighteen and twenty who meet other requirements for office are eligible for election to any office that does not require a minimum age (Attorney General's Opinion 46, October 12, 1971).

Given that Article 2, section 1 requires electors to be U.S. citizens, aliens are not eligible to hold public office (Attorney General's Opinion 356, December 17, 1954).

A convicted felon is not a qualified elector under Article 2, section 1. Even a felon who has been "released from the penalties and disabilities of his crime" does not automatically reacquire his or her lost civil rights. A convicted felon who has not been restored to civil rights "may not vote, hold office, or serve as a juror" (Attorney General's Opinion 83-13, September 14, 1983).

Sec: 4. **Perpetuities; eleemosynary purposes**

No perpetuities shall be allowed except for eleemosynary purposes.

The limitation on perpetuities established by this section applies only to private trusts, not public or charitable trusts. The term *eleemosynary* is synonymous with *charitable*. In order for a trust to be deemed charitable, it must have "a donor, . . . a trustee competent to take, . . . a use restricted to a charitable purpose, . . . and a definite beneficiary" (*Nixon v. Brown*).

Sec: 5. **Time of general election**

The general election shall be held on the Tuesday next after the first Monday of November.

There has been no interpretation of this section.

Sec: 6. **Number of members of legislature limited**

The aggregate number of members of both branches of the Legislature shall never exceed Seventy five.

In *Dungan v. Sawyer*, a federal court held that this section would violate the U.S. Constitution "only if, and to the extent, that it prohibits the creation of a valid and lawful plan of apportionment." Article 4, section 5 further requires that of this number, the senate must be "not less than one-third nor more than one-half" the size of the assembly.

Sec: 7. **County offices at county seats**

All county Officers shall hold their Offices at the County seat of their respective Counties.

This section prohibits county officers from maintaining other offices outside the county seat even if their principal office is at the county seat (Attorney General's Opinion 155, March 19, 1956).

Sec: 8. **Publication of general statutes and opinions of supreme court; effective date of opinions of supreme court**

The Legislature shall provide for the speedy publication of all Statute laws of a general nature, and such decisions of the Supreme Court, as it may

> deem expedient; and all laws and judicial decisions shall be free for pub-
> lication by any person; *Provided*, that no judgment of the Supreme Court
> shall take effect and be operative until the Opinion of the Court in such case
> shall be filed with the Clerk of said Court.

This section has not been subject to significant interpretation.

Sec: 9. **Increase or decrease of compensation of officers whose compensation is fixed by constitution**

> The Legislature may, at any time, provide by law for increasing or dimin-
> ishing the salaries or compensation of any of the Officers, whose salaries
> or compensation is fixed in this Constitution; Provided, no such change of
> Salary or compensation shall apply to any Officer during the term for which
> he may have been elected.

This section prohibits the legislature from increasing or decreasing the salaries of the officers noted in Article 17, section 5 before they have stood for election. The supreme court has liberally construed section 9 to imply that ambiguous statutes that give the authority to fix compensation should be read to deny the legislature the power to alter salaries before an election has occurred (*Cannon v. Taylor*).

Officers who were originally included in Article 17, section 5 but whose positions have since become appointive instead of elective (e.g., superintendent of public instruction; see Article 11, section 1) are no longer within the scope of this section.

County officers are not included in this section's prohibition and may have their salaries changed during their term of office (*State ex rel. Miller v. Lani*). Nor does this section apply to township officers or state officers created by statute (Attorney General's Opinion, March 7, 1910).

An individual holding two offices (e.g., secretary of state and ex officio clerk of the supreme court) is entitled to the compensation provided for both offices (*State ex rel. Howell v. LaGrave*).

Sec: 10. **Election or appointment of officers**

> All officers whose election or appointment is not otherwise provided for,
> shall be chose nor appointed as may be prescribed by law.

This provision has been construed to give the legislature broad power to provide for the selection of other officers. The power to fill these offices is not a part of the governor's power as chief executive, and the legislature may provide for the appointment of railroad commissioners by the governor, lieutenant governor, and attorney general (*Southern Pacific Company v. Bartine*) or for the selection of state board members by other members of the board (Attorney General's

Opinion 611, August 28, 1969). However, any officers for whom election is the constitutionally prescribed method of selection (e.g., county assessors) must be elected. The legislature may not provide any other means to fill these offices (*State ex rel. Perry v. Arrington*).

Sec: 11. **Term of office when not fixed by constitution; limitation; municipal officers and employees**

> The tenure of any office not herein provided for may be declared by law, or, when not so declared, such office shall be held during the pleasure of the authority making the appointment, but the legislature shall not create any office the tenure of which shall be longer than four (4) years, except as herein otherwise provided in this constitution. In the case of any officer or employee of any municipality governed under a legally adopted charter, the provisions of such charter with reference to the tenure of office or the dismissal from office of any such officer or employee shall control.

The last sentence of this section was added in 1946 to give chartered municipalities control over the terms of their officers and employees. When a charter or law does not specify a term of office, the officeholder serves at the will of the appointing authority and may be removed without any reason being given (*Leeper v. Jamison; Eads v. City of Boulder City*).

The legislature may provide for terms of longer than four years for offices created by the constitution but for which it has not fixed a term; however, offices created by the legislature cannot have a term exceeding four years (Attorney General's Opinion 326, March 15, 1929). Should the legislature improperly create an office with a term more than four years, the office is valid, but the elected official may legally serve only four years of this term (Attorney General's Opinion 326, March 15, 1929; Attorney General's Opinion A-4, February 28, 1939).

Sec: 12. **Certain state officers to keep offices at Carson City**

> The Governor, Secretary of State, State Treasurer, State Controller, and Clerk of the Supreme Court, shall keep their respective offices at the seat of Government.

There has been no significant interpretation of this section.

Sec: 13. **Census by legislature and congress: Basis of representation in houses of legislature**

> The enumeration of the inhabitants in this State shall be taken under the direction of the Legislature if deemed necessary in A.D. Eighteen hundred

and Sixty five, A.D. Eighteen hundred and Sixty seven, A.D. Eighteen
hundred and Seventy five and every ten years thereafter; and these enumerations, together with the census that may be taken under the direction
of the Congress of the United States in A.D. Eighteen hundred and Seventy,
and every subsequent ten years shall serve as the basis of representation in
both houses of the Legislature.

Between 1915 and 1965, Nevada was in violation of this section and Article 1,
section 13 requiring apportionment on the basis of population. During that time,
the state adopted by statute an apportionment of one senator per county. In 1950
Article 4, section 5, but not Articles 1 or 15, was amended in a questionable
attempt to legitimize this "little federal" plan.

The U.S. Supreme Court's decision in *Reynolds v. Sims* that these schemes
violated the U.S. Constitution led a three-judge federal court to declare Nevada's
apportionment unconstitutional (*Dungan v. Sawyer*), and in 1970 Article 4 was
amended once more to return to the intent of the drafters of the original constitution that the state's citizens should have "an equal representation in making
the laws of the state—one of the most sacred rights of citizenship—a right to
be enjoyed equally by all the citizens of the state" (*State ex rel. Winnie v.
Stoddard*).

Sec: 14. Election by plurality

A plurality of votes given at an election by the people, shall constitute a
choice, where not otherwise provided by this Constitution.

Although many states, especially in the South, require runoff elections when no
one candidate receives a majority vote, this section and Article 5, section 4 note
that, except where provided otherwise by the state constitution, the candidate
with the most votes wins election even if he or she does not have a majority.
This section has not been subject to interpretation.

Sec: 15. Merit system governing employment in executive branch

The legislature shall provide by law for a state merit system governing the
employment of employees in the executive branch of state government.

Section 15 was added by constitutional amendment in 1970, forcing the legislature to provide for a competitive civil service system in the state in order to
eliminate vestiges of patronage in the executive branch. It has not been subject
to interpretation.

Article 16

Amendments

Sec: 1. **Constitutional amendments: Procedure; concurrent and consecutive amendments**

Any amendment or amendments to this Constitution may be proposed in the Senate or Assembly; and if the same shall be agreed to by a Majority of all the members elected to each of the two houses, such proposed amendment or amendments shall be entered on their respective journals, with the Yeas and Nays taken thereon, and referred to the Legislature then next to be chosen, and shall be published for three months next preceding the time of making such choice. And if in the Legislature next chosen as aforesaid, such proposed amendment or amendments shall be agreed to by a majority of all the members elected to each house, then it shall be the duty of the Legislature to submit such proposed amendment or amendments to the people, in such manner and at such time as the Legislature shall prescribe; and if the people shall approve and ratify such amendment or amendments by a majority of the electors qualified to vote for members of the Legislature voting thereon, such amendment or amendments shall, unless precluded by subsection 2, become a part of the Constitution.

Amendment of the Nevada Constitution can occur by no method other than that provided in the constitution itself (*State ex rel. Stevenson v. Tufly*).

Prior to the addition in 1912 of the initiative process in Article 19, the sole method for amending the constitution was the approval by two sessions of the legislature and ratification by the voters at an election. In the same manner as other legislation, the proposal must be passed by a majority of the total membership of each house and not just those present. However, only a simple majority of those voting on the question, *not* a majority of the total vote cast in an election, is necessary for ratification (Attorney General's Opinion 273, March 8, 1939).

Three amendments approved by the voters in 1886 and ten approved in 1888 were held inoperable by the supreme court for failure to enter them in the legislative journals. The amendments do not have to be entered in full in the journals; an identifying reference is sufficient (*Ex parte Ming*).

Publication of an amendment is required at least three months preceding an election in order to allow the voters an opportunity to discuss it. The legislature has the discretion to determine whether the manner of publication shall be in newspapers or the statutes (*State ex rel. Torreyson v. Grey*).

Adopted amendments become effective upon the canvass of votes by the Supreme Court (*Torvinen v. Rollins*).

> 2. If two or more amendments which affect the same section of the constitution are ratified by the people at the same election:
>
> (a) If all can be given effect without contradiction in substance, each shall become a part of the constitution.
>
> (b) If one or more contradict in substance the other or others, that amendment which received the largest favorable vote, and any other amendment or amendments compatible with it, shall become a part of the constitution.

Paragraph 2 was added in 1972 to deal with the possibility of two or more conflicting amendments being ratified in the same general election. The potential for this kind of problem was increased with the addition of the initiative process in 1912 since an initiative proposal and legislative proposal or two initiative proposals in conflict might be on the same ballot. In that case, the proposal gaining the most positive votes would be adopted; a conflicting one with fewer positive votes, even though approved, would not. This section has not been subject to legal interpretation.

> 3. If after the proposal of an amendment, another amendment is ratified which affects the same section of the constitution but is compatible with the proposed amendment, the next legislature if it agrees to the proposed amendment shall submit such proposal to the people as a further amendment to the amended section. If, after the proposal of an amendment, another amendment is ratified which contradicts in substance the proposed amendment, such proposed amendment shall not be submitted to the people.

Paragraph 3 was also added in 1972 to stop legislative proposals for amendment prior to their appearance on an election ballot if they conflict with an amendment ratified during the proposal process. This paragraph has not been subject to legal interpretation.

Sec: 2. **Convention for revision of constitution: Procedure**

> If at any time the Legislature by a vote of two thirds of the Members elected
> to each house, shall determine that it is necessary to cause a revision of this
> entire Constitution they shall recommend to the electors at the next election
> for Members of the Legislature, to vote for or against a convention, and if
> it shall appear that a majority of the electors voting at such election, shall
> have voted in favor of calling a Convention to be holden [*sic*] within six
> months after the passage of such law, and such Convention shall consist of
> a number of members not less than that of both branches of the Legislature.
> In determining what is a majority of the electors voting at such election,
> reference shall be had to the highest number of votes cast at such election
> for the candidates for any office or on any question.

Some state constitutions (e.g., Illinois) require a periodic submission to the voters on the question of revising or writing an entirely new constitution. Nevada does not, and the process of revision is, understandably, more difficult than mere amendment. A convention to revise the constitution can be called only upon the approval of two-thirds of the total membership of each house of the legislature and a majority of the voters at a general election.

A proposal to call for a constitutional convention has appeared on the ballot four times: 1876, 1884, 1888, and 1890. The proposal failed the first three times but apparently passed in 1890; however, through various legislative maneuvers and allegations of defective ballots, the state legislature never called the convention.[28]

Although this section has not been subject to judicial interpretation, it is clear from its plain words, the debates of the 1864 convention, and the deliberately difficult nature of the revision process that a ballot question to call a constitutional convention would require a majority of the total votes cast in a general election and not simply a majority of those voting on the question. Thus, those who vote in the general election but fail to vote on the convention question would be counted as "no" votes.

Section 2 is silent on the question of whether a new constitution requires the ratification of the voters. Although the issue was not discussed at all in the 1864 convention, given the experiences of other states and the original requirement in the congressional enabling act for a ratification vote of the 1864 constitution, it is probable that the revised constitution would have to be approved by the state's voters. It would be strange indeed that a mere constitutional amendment would require voter ratification, while an entirely new constitution would not.

Article 17

Schedule

Article 17 appears, at first glance, to be of only historical value as a set of rules and regulations governing the transition from territorial status to statehood. For most sections, that is true. However, the courts have held this schedule to be of "continuing vitality" in that some of "its provisions may still be made applicable" (*State ex rel. Herr v. Laxalt*). Those that are of "continuing vitality" are discussed below; the others are presented for their historical value.

Sec: 1. Saving existing rights and liabilities

That no inconvenience may arise by reason of a change from a Territorial to a permanent State Government, it is declared, that all rights, actions, prosecutions, judgments, Claims and Contracts, as well of individuals, as of bodies corporate, including counties, towns and cities, shall continue as if no change had taken place; and all process which may issue under the Authority of the Territory of Nevada, previous to its admission into the Union as one of the United States, shall be as valid as if issued in the name of the State of Nevada.

Sec: 2. Territorial laws to remain in force

All laws of the Territory of Nevada in force at the time of the admission of this State, not repugnant to this Constitution, shall remain in force until they expire by their own limitations or be altered or repealed by the Legislature.

Alteration of a section of a territorial law does not repeal the law in its entirety; territorial laws remain in force unless repealed or modified by the constitution or legislation (*Bowers v. Beck*).

Sec: 3. **Fines, penalties, and forfeitures to inure to state**

All fines, penalties and forfeitures accruing to the Territory of Nevada or to the people of the United States in the Territory of Nevada, shall inure to the State of Nevada.

Sec: 4. **Existing obligations and pending suits**

All recognizances heretofore taken, or which may be taken before the change from a Territorial, to a State Government, shall remain valid, and shall pass to, and may be prosecuted in the name of the State, and all bonds, executed to the Governor of the Territory or to any other Officer or Court in his or their official capacity, or to the people of the United States in the Territory of Nevada, shall pass to the Governor, or other officer or court, and his or their successors in office for the uses therein respectively expressed, and may be sued on, and recovery had accordingly; And all property real, personal or mixed, and all judgements [*sic*], bonds, specialties, choses in Action, claims and debts of whatsoever description, and records, and public Archives of the Territory of Nevada, shall issue to and vest in the State of Nevada, and may be sued for and recovered in the same manner and to the same extent by the State of Nevada, as the same could have been by the Territory of Nevada. All criminal prosecutions and penal Actions, which may have arisen, or which may arise before the change from a Territorial to a State Government, and which shall then be pending, shall be prosecuted to judgement [*sic*] and execution in the name of the State. All offenses committed against the laws of the Territory of Nevada, before the change from a Territorial to a State Government, and which shall not be prosecuted before such change, may be prosecuted in the name and by the Authority of the State of Nevada, with like effect as though such change had not taken place; And all penalties incurred, shall remain the same as if this Constitution had not been adopted; All actions at law, and suits in equity, and other legal proceedings, which may be pending in any of the Courts of the Territory of Nevada at the time of the change from a Territorial to a State Government may be continued and transferred to, and determined by, any court of the State, which shall have jurisdiction of the subject matter thereof. All actions at law and suits in Equity, and all other legal proceedings, which may be pending in any of the Courts of the Territory of Nevada at the time of the change from a Territorial to a State Government, shall be continued and transferred to, and may be prosecuted to judgement [*sic*] and execution in any Court of the State which shall have jurisdiction of the subject matter thereof; And all books, papers and records, relating to the same shall be transferred in like manner to such court.

Sec: 5. Salaries of state officers for first term of office

For the first term of office succeeding the formation of a State Government, the Salary of the Governor shall be Four Thousand Dollars per annum; The salary of the Secretary of State shall be Three Thousand, Six hundred Dollars per annum; The salary of the State Controller shall be Three Thousand, Six hundred Dollars per annum; The salary of the State Treasurer shall be Three Thousand Six hundred Dollars per Annum; The salary of the Surveyor General shall be One Thousand Dollars per annum; The salary of the Attorney General shall be Two Thousand Five hundred Dollars per annum; The salary of the Superintendent of Public Instruction shall be Two Thousand Dollars per annum; The salary of each judge of the Supreme Court shall be Seven Thousand Dollars per annum; The salaries of the foregoing officers, shall be paid quarterly, out of the State Treasury. The pay of State Senators and Members of the Assembly shall be Eight Dollars per day, for each day of actual service, and forty cents per mile for mileage going to, and returning from, the place of meeting. No officer mentioned in this Section, shall receive any fee or perquisites, to his own use for the performance of any duty connected with his office, or for the performance of any additional duty imposed upon him by law.

Sec: 6. Apportionment of senators and assemblymen

Until otherwise provided by Law the apportionment of Senators and Assemblymen in the different counties shall be as follows, to Wit: Storey County four Senators and Twelve Assemblymen, Douglas County One Senator and Two Assemblymen; Esmeralda County, Two Senators and Four Assemblymen; Humboldt County, Two Senators and Three Assemblymen, Lander County Two Senators and Four Assemblymen; Lyon County, One Senator and Three Assemblymen; Lyon and Churchill Counties, One Senator jointly; Churchill County One Assemblyman; Nye County One Senator and one Assemblyman; Ormsby County Two Senators and Three Assemblymen; Washoe and Roop Counties, Two Senators and Three Assemblymen.

Sec: 7. Assumption of territorial debts and liabilities

All debts and liabilities of the Territory of Nevada, lawfully incurred and which remain unpaid, at the time of admission of this State into the Union shall be assumed by and become the debt of the State of Nevada; Provided that the assumption of such indebtedness shall not prevent the State from contracting the additional indebtedness as provided in Section Three of Article Nine of this Constitution.

Sec: 8. Terms of elected state officers

The term of State Officers, except Judicial, elected at the first election under this Constitution shall continue until the Tuesday after the first Monday of

January A.D. Eighteen hundred and sixty seven, and until the election and qualification of their successors.

Sec: 9. **Terms of senators**

The Senators to be elected at the first election under this Constitution shall draw lots, so that, the term of one half of the number as nearly as may be, shall expire on the day succeeding the general election in A.D. Eighteen Hundred and Sixty Six; and the term of the other half shall expire on the day succeeding the general election in A.D. Eighteen hundred and sixty eight, Provided, that in drawing lots for all Senatorial terms, the Senatorial representation shall be allotted, so that in the Counties having two or more Senators, the terms thereof shall be divided as nearly as may be between the long and short terms.

Sec: 10. **Terms of senators and assemblymen after 1866**

At the general election in A.D. Eighteen hundred and Sixty Six; and thereafter, the term of Senators shall be for Four Years from the day succeeding such general election, and members of Assembly for Two Years from the day succeeding such general election, and the terms of Senators shall be allotted by the Legislature in long and short terms as hereinbefore provided; so that one half the number as nearly as may be, shall be elected every Two Years.

Should the state legislature choose to increase the size of the state senate, as it has on several occasions, it has "continuing authority" under this section to allot short and long initial terms of office but "only when such action is necessary to provide for the election of one-half of their number every 2 years" (*State ex rel. Herr v. Laxalt*).

Sec: 11. **Terms of assemblymen: Elected at first general election and in 1865**

The term of the members of the Assembly elected at the first general election under this Constitution shall expire on the day succeeding the general election in A.D. Eighteen hundred and Sixty Five; and the terms of those elected at the general election in A.D. Eighteen hundred and Sixty Five, shall expire on the day succeeding the general election in A.D. Eighteen hundred and Sixty six.

Sec: 12. **First biennial legislative session to commence in 1867**

The first regular session of the Legislature shall commence on the second Monday of December A.D. Eighteen hundred and Sixty Four, and the second

regular session of the same shall commence on the first Monday of January
A.D. Eighteen hundred and Sixty Six; and the third regular session of the
Legislature shall be the first of the biennial sessions, and shall commence
on the first Monday of January A.D. Eighteen hundred and Sixty Seven; and
the regular sessions of the Legislature shall be held thereafter biennially,
commencing on the first Monday of January.

Sec: 13. Continuation of territorial county and township officers; probate judges

All county officers under the laws of the Territory of Nevada at the time
when the Constitution shall take effect, whose offices are not inconsistent
with the provisions of this Constitution, shall continue in office until the
first Monday of January A.D. Eighteen hundred and Sixty Seven, and until
their successors are elected and qualified; and all township officers shall
continue in office until the expiration of their terms of office, and until their
successors are elected and qualified; Provided, that the Probate Judges of
the several counties respectively, shall continue in office until the election
and qualification of the District Judges of the several counties or Judicial
Districts; And Provided further, that the term of office of the present county
officers of Lander County, shall expire on the first Monday of January A.D.
Eighteen hundred and Sixty Five, except the Probate Judge of said County
whose term of office shall expire upon the first Monday of December A.D.
Eighteen hundred and Sixty Four, and there shall be an election for County
Officers of Lander County at the general election in November A.D. Eighteen
hundred and Sixty Four, and the officers then elected, shall hold office from
the first Monday of January A.D. Eighteen hundred and Sixty five until the
first Monday of January A.D. Eighteen hundred and sixty seven, and until
their successors are elected and qualified.

Sec: 14. Duties of certain territorial officers continued

The Governor, Secretary, Treasurer and Superintendent of Public Instruction
of the Territory of Nevada shall each continue to discharge the duties of
their respective offices after the admission of this State into the Union, and
until the time designated for the qualification of the above named officers
to be elected under the State Government, and the Territorial Auditor shall
continue to discharge the duties of his said office until the time appointed
for the qualification of the State Controller; Provided, that the said officers
shall each receive the salaries, and be subject to the restrictions and conditions
provided in this Constitution; and Provided further, that none of them shall
receive to his own use any fees or perquisites for the performance of any
duty connected with his office.

Sec: 15. **Terms of supreme court and district courts**

The terms of the Supreme Court shall, until provision be made by law, be held at such times as the Judges of the said Court or a majority of them may appoint. The first terms of the several District Courts (except as here-inafter mentioned) shall commence on the first Monday of December A.D. Eighteen Hundred and Sixty Four. The first term of the District Court of the Fifth Judicial District, shall commence on the first Monday of December A.D Eighteen Hundred and Sixty Four in the County of Nye; and shall commence on the first Monday of January A.D. Eighteen Hundred and Sixty Five in the County of Churchill. The terms of the Fourth Judicial District Court shall until otherwise provided by law be held at the County Seat of Washoe County, and the first term thereof commence on the first Monday of December, A.D. Eighteen Hundred and Sixty Four.

Sec: 16. **Salaries of district judges**

The Judges of the several District Courts of this State shall be paid as hereinbefore provided Salaries at the following rates per Annum: First Judicial District (Each Judge) Six Thousand Dollars; Second Judicial District Four Thousand Dollars; Third Judicial District, Five Thousand Dollars; Fourth Judicial District Five Thousand Dollars; Fifth Judicial District Thirty Six Hundred Dollars; Sixth Judicial District Four Thousand Dollars; Seventh Judicial District Six Thousand Dollars; Eighth Judicial District Thirty Six Hundred Dollars; Ninth Judicial District Five Thousand Dollars.

Sec: 17. **Alteration of salary of district judge authorized**

The salary of any Judge in said Judicial Districts may by law be altered or changed, subject to the provisions contained in this Constitution.

Sec: 18. **Qualification and terms of certain elective state officers**

The Governor, Lieutenant Governor, Secretary of State, State Treasurer, State Controller, Attorney General, Surveyor General, Clerk of the Supreme Court and Superintendent of Public Instruction, to be elected at the first election under this Constitution shall each qualify and enter upon the duties of their respective offices on the first Monday of December succeeding their election and shall continue in office until the first Tuesday after the first Monday of January A.D. Eighteen hundred and Sixty Seven, and until the election and qualification of their successors respectively.

Sec: 19. **When justices of supreme court and district judges enter upon duties**

The Judges of the Supreme Court and District Judges to be elected at the first election under this Constitution shall qualify and enter upon the duties of their respective offices on the first Monday of December succeeding their election.

Sec: 20. **State officers and district judges to be commissioned by territorial governor; state controller and treasurer to furnish bonds**

All officers of State, and District Judges first elected under this Constitution shall be commissioned by the Governor of this Territory, which commission shall be countersigned by the Secretary of the same, and shall qualify before entering upon the discharge of their duties, before any officer authorized to administer oaths under the Laws of this Territory; and also the State Controller and State Treasurer shall each respectively, before they qualify, and enter upon the discharge of their duties, execute and deliver to the Secretary of the Territory of Nevada an Official Bond, made payable to the People of the State of Nevada in the sum of Thirty Thousand Dollars, to be approved by the Governor of the Territory of Nevada; and shall also execute and deliver to the Secretary of State such other or further official Bond or Bonds as may be required by law.

Sec: 21. **Support of county and city officers**

Each County, Town, City, and Incorporated Village shall make provision for the support of its own officers, subject to such regulations as may be prescribed by law.

This section does not prohibit the legislature from changing the compensation or fees of a county officer during his or her term of office (Attorney General's Opinion, May 29, 1899).

Sec: 22. **Vacancies in certain state offices: How filled**

In case the office of any State officer, except a judicial officer, shall become vacant before the expiration of the regular term for which he was elected, the vacancy may be filled by appointment by the Governor until it shall be supplied at the next general election, when it shall be filled by election for the residue of the unexpired term.

The exception for judicial officers was added in 1976 as part of the amendment creating a commission on judicial selection in Article 6, section 20 to fill judicial vacancies through a modified merit plan. Prior to that time, judicial vacancies were filled by the governor in the same manner as other vacancies in state office continue to be filled: gubernatorial appointment until the next general election, when candidates may run for the remainder of the term. New state offices created by the legislature must also be filled in this way prior to election and not by the legislature itself (*State ex rel. Dickerson v. Elwell*).

Sec: 23. **Civil and criminal cases pending in probate courts transferred to district courts**

All cases both civil and criminal, which may be pending and undetermined in the Probate Courts of the several counties at the time when under the provisions of this Constitution, said Probate Courts are to be abolished, shall be transferred to and determined by the District Courts of such counties respectively.

Sec: 24. **Levy of tax limited for 3 years**

For the first Three Years after the adoption of this Constitution the Legislature shall not levy a tax for State purposes, exceeding one per cent per annum on the taxable property in the State, Provided, the Legislature may levy a special tax not exceeding one fourth of one per cent per annum, which shall be appropriated to the payment of indebtedness of the Territory of Nevada, assumed by the State of Nevada, and for that purpose only, until all of said indebtedness is paid.

Sec: 25. **Roop County attached to Washoe County**

The County of Roop shall be attached to the County of Washoe for Judicial, Legislative, Revenue and County purposes, until otherwise provided by law.

Sec: 26. **Constitutional debates and proceedings: Publication; payment of reporter**

At the first regular session of the Legislature to convene under the requirements of this Constitution, provisions shall be made by law for paying for the publication of Six Hundred copies of the Debates and proceedings of this Convention in Book form, to be disposed of as the Legislature may direct; and the Hon. J. Neeley Johnson President of this Convention, shall contract for, and A. J. Marsh, official reporter of this convention under the direction of the President, shall supervise the publication of such debates and proceedings. Provision shall be made by law, at such first session of the Legislature for the compensation of the official reporter of this convention, and he shall be paid in coin or its equivalent. He shall receive for his services in reporting the debates and proceedings, Fifteen Dollars per day during the session of the Convention, and Seven and one half dollars additional for each evening session, and thirty cents per folio of one hundred words for preparing the same for publication, and for supervising and indexing such publication the sum of Fifteen Dollars per day during the time actually engaged in such service.

Article 18

Right of Suffrage

Rights of suffrage and officeholding

[Repealed in 1992.]

Prior to its repeal in 1992, this article stated, "The rights of suffrage and officeholding shall not be withheld from any male citizen of the United States by reason of his color or previous condition of servitude." It was added in 1880 in order to bring the state's constitution into compliance with the U.S. Constitution's Fifteenth Amendment, ratified in 1870, prohibiting the denial of the right to vote on the basis of "race, color, or previous condition of servitude." It was repealed by the voters on the basis that it had become obsolete since voting and officeholding rights are guaranteed to all adult citizens, regardless of race or gender, by various amendments adopted since that time to the U.S. Constitution (e.g., the Nineteenth Amendment) and the Nevada Constitution's Article 2, section 1, and Article 15, section 3.

Article 19

Initiative and Referendum

Sec: 1. **Referendum for approval or disapproval of statute or resolution enacted by legislature**

1. A person who intends to circulate a petition that a statute or part thereof enacted by the legislature be submitted to a vote of the people, before circulating the petition for signatures, shall file a copy thereof with the secretary of state. He shall file the copy not earlier than August 1 of the year before the year in which the election will be held.

2. Whenever a number of registered voters of this state equal to 10 percent or more of the number of voters who voted at the last preceding general election shall express their wish by filing with the secretary of state, not less than 120 days before the next general election, a petition in the form provided for in section 3 of this article that any statute or resolution or any part thereof enacted by the legislature be submitted to a vote of the people, the officers charged with the duties of announcing and proclaiming elections and of certifying nominations or questions to be voted upon shall submit the question of approval or disapproval of such statute or resolution or any part thereof to a vote of the voters at the next succeeding election at which such question may be voted upon by the registered voters of the entire state. The circulation of the petition shall cease on the day the petition is filed with the secretary of state or such other date as may be prescribed for the verification of the number of signatures affixed to the petition, whichever is earliest.

3. If a majority of voters voting upon the proposal submitted at such election votes approval of such statute or resolution or any part thereof, such statute or resolution or any part thereof shall stand as the law of the state and shall not be amended, annulled, repealed, set aside, suspended or in

any way made inoperative except by the direct vote of the people. If a
majority of such voters votes disapproval of such statute or resolution or
any part thereof, such statute or resolution or any part thereof shall be void
and of no effect.

This section establishing the Progressive era direct democracy process of referendum was added in 1904 and amended in 1962 and 1988. Referendum, which
gives the voters an opportunity to negate or approve of a legislative enactment,
has been used sparingly in the state. Only "legislative" and not "administrative"
matters can be referred to the voters. An action "originating or enacting a
permanent law or laying down a rule of conduct or course of policy" is legislative
in character and can be referred; an ordinance that "simply puts into execution
previously-declared policies or previously-enacted laws" is administrative and
cannot be referred to the voters (*Forman v. Eagle Thrifty Drugs & Markets,
Inc.*).

Prior to the 1962 amendment, a referendum had to receive a majority of the
votes cast in an election, not just a majority of those voting on the question.
Since 1962, however, only a majority of those voting on the question is required
to approve or disapprove a legislative enactment.

An interesting aspect of the Nevada referendum process is that a law approved
by referendum initiated by the people cannot be amended or repealed by the
legislature; change or repeal could occur only by another direct vote of the
people. This provision led pro-choice forces in Nevada to put the statutes on
abortion up for a referendum vote in 1990. These statutes, which enacted into
law the guidelines established by the U.S. Supreme Court's decision in *Roe v.
Wade*, were approved in the referendum; thus, even if the Court were to overturn
Roe, pro-life forces could not prohibit the right to abortion without another costly
and time-consuming referendum.

This prohibition on amending or repealing a referendum-approved statute
applies only if the referendum was initiated by the people. Issues referred by
the legislature to a referendum vote by its power under Article 4, section 1 can
be subsequently amended or repealed by the legislature because these statutes
do not possess Article 19 immunity (Attorney General's Opinion 190, May 15,
1975).

The filing of a referendum petition does not have the effect of suspending the
operation of the law until the election (*State ex rel. Morton v. Howard*); however,
a statute that is repealed becomes void immediately upon the official canvass of
the vote (Attorney General's Opinion 382, August 5, 1930).

Sec: 2. Initiative petition for enactment or amendment of statute or amendment of constitution

1. Notwithstanding the provisions of section 1 of article 4 of this constitution, but subject to the limitations of section 6 of this article, the people

> reserve to themselves the power to propose, by initiative petition, statutes
> and amendments to statutes and amendments to this constitution, and to
> enact or reject them at the polls.

This section establishing the initiative, also a Progressive era direct democracy reform, was added in 1912 and has been amended seven times since. Prior to that time, only the legislature could enact statutes (see Article 4) and propose constitutional amendments (see Article 16). Initiative allows the people to propose and enact legislation and constitutional amendments "independent of the legislature" (*Wilson v. Koontz*). Although the power of initiative is "extremely broad" (*Forman v. Eagle Thrifty Drugs & Markets, Inc.*), it, too, has been used sparingly in Nevada.

In practicing initiative, the people have the same sovereignty as the legislature and are "bound by the same constitutional limitations and restrictions" (Attorney General's Opinion 153, December 21, 1934). Thus, the courts retain the power to enjoin submission to the voters of an initiative that would "palpably violate the paramount law and would inevitably be futile and nugatory and incapable of being made operative under any conditions or circumstances" (*Caine v. Robbins; Stumpf v. Lau*).[29]

> 2. An initiative petition shall be in the form required by section 3 of this
> article and shall be proposed by a number of registered voters equal to 10
> percent or more of the number of voters who voted at the last preceding
> general election in not less than 75 percent of the counties in the state, but
> the total number of registered voters signing the initiative petition shall be
> equal to 10 percent or more of the voters who voted in the entire state at
> the last preceding general election.

Unlike the referendum petition, which requires the signatures of 10 percent of the number of voters who voted in the state's previous general election, the initiative petition requires the signatures of 10 percent of the number of voters voting in the previous general election in 75 percent or more of the state's counties. With Nevada's current seventeen counties, an initiative petition is required to have the signatures of 10 percent of the voters in at least thirteen counties who voted in the previous general election. This requirement has the effect of preventing the voters in the state's two most populous counties (Clark and Washoe) from putting an initiative on the ballot without support from at least eleven of the so-called cow counties. The total number of signatures on the petition must also be equal to at least 10 percent of those in the entire state voting in the previous general election.

In *Moore v. Ogilvie* the U.S. Supreme Court held unconstitutional a geographical dispersion requirement mandating that a candidate in Illinois obtain at least 200 signatures in 50 of the state's 102 counties in order to have his or her name placed on the ballot. The geographical dispersion requirement of section 2 would appear to be similarly handicapped. In an opinion by Nevada's attorney general, however, it was held that the "one person, one vote" rule does not apply to the initiative petition process. That opinion noted that "*introducing* and *enacting* legislation are two different things," and just as a legislative committee introducing legislation in the state legislature might be overrepresentative of sparsely populated counties, the actual enactment of such legislation would require that all members of a constitutionally apportioned legislature be allowed to vote on it. Similarly, the process of introduction by initiative petition might be overrepresentative of the cow counties, but enactment would require that all voters in the state be allowed to vote on the issue (Attorney General's Opinion 188, April 18, 1975). The Nevada courts have not ruled on the issue.

    3. If the initiative petition proposes a statute or amendment to a statute, the person who intends to circulate it shall file a copy with the secretary of state before beginning circulation and not earlier than January 1 of the year preceding the year in which a regular session of the legislature is held. After its circulation, it shall be filed with the secretary of state not less than 30 days prior to any regular session of the legislature. The circulation of the petition shall cease on the day the petition is filed with the secretary of state or such other date as may be prescribed for the verification of the number of signatures affixed to the petition, whichever is earliest. The secretary of state shall transmit such petition to the legislature as soon as the legislature convenes and organizes. The petition shall take precedence over all other matters except appropriation bills, and the statute or amendment to a statute proposed thereby shall be enacted or rejected by the legislature without change or amendment within 40 days. If the proposed statute or amendment to a statute is enacted by the legislature and approved by the governor in the same manner as other statutes are enacted, such statute or amendment to a statute shall become law, but shall be subject to referendum petition as provided in section 1 of this article. If the statute or amendment to a statute is rejected by the legislature, or if no action is taken thereon within 40 days, the secretary of state shall submit the question of approval or disapproval of such statute or amendment to a statute to a vote of the voters at the next succeeding general election. If a majority of the voters voting on such question at such election votes approval of such statute or amendment to a statute, it shall become law and take effect upon completion of the canvass of votes by the supreme court. An initiative measure so approved by the voters shall not be amended, annulled, repealed, set aside or suspended by the legislature within 3 years from the date it takes effect. If a majority of such voters votes disapproval of such statute or amendment to a statute, no further action shall be taken on such petition. If the legislature rejects such proposed statute or amendment, the governor may recommend to the legislature and the legislature may propose a different measure on the same subject, in which event, after such different measure has been approved by the governor, the question of approval of each measure shall be submitted by the secretary of state to a vote of the voters at the next succeeding general election. If the conflicting provisions submitted to the voters are both approved by a majority of the voters voting on such measures, the measure

which receives the largest number of affirmative votes shall thereupon become law.

The initiative process can be used to enact a statute or to amend the constitution. These two types of initiative are dealt with separately. Section 2, paragraph 3 details the appropriate process for a proposed statute, and paragraph 4 establishes guidelines for a proposed constitutional amendment. Prior to the 1962 amendment to Article 19, all initiatives, whether proposed statutes or constitutional amendments, were treated the same as proposed statutes are currently: submission to the legislature and approval at a single general election.

A proposed statute that receives the appropriate number of signatures must be transmitted by the secretary of state to both houses of the state legislature (Attorney General's Opinion 12, February 6, 1917). The legislature then has forty days from the start of its session to act upon the petition. If the legislature approves and the governor signs it, the proposed statute becomes law. If the legislature and governor disapprove or do nothing, the measure will go on the next general election ballot for approval or disapproval by the voters.

Approval by the voters requires a majority of those voting on the question, and such approval immunizes the statute from change or repeal by the legislature for a period of three years, unlike referendum-approved statutes, which have complete immunity from legislative change (see section 2, paragraph 3). These statutes are effective immediately upon the official canvass of votes by the state supreme court and are "subject to the same rules of statutory interpretation as acts passed directly by the Legislature" (Attorney General's Opinion 407, September 22, 1958).

If the legislature or governor disapproves of a statute proposed by initiative, they may pass an alternative that will also be placed on the ballot with the original proposition. The proposition winning the most affirmative votes becomes law.

4. If the initiative petition proposes an amendment to the constitution, the person who intends to circulate it shall file a copy with the secretary of state before beginning circulation and not earlier than September 1 of the year before the year in which the election is to be held. After its circulation it shall be filed with the secretary of state not less than 90 days before any regular general election at which the question of approval or disapproval of such amendment may be voted upon by the voters of the entire state. The circulation of the petition shall cease on the day the petition is filed with the secretary of state or such other date as may be prescribed for the verification of the number of signatures affixed to the petition, whichever is earliest. The secretary of state shall cause to be published in a newspaper of general circulation, on three separate occasions, in each county in the state, together with any explanatory matter which shall be placed upon the ballot, the entire text of the proposed amendment. If a majority of the voters voting on such questions at such election votes disapproval of such amend-

ment, no further action shall be taken on the petition. If a majority of such voters votes approval of such amendment, the secretary of state shall publish and resubmit the question of approval or disapproval to a vote of the voters at the next succeeding general election in the same manner as such question was originally submitted. If a majority of such voters votes disapproval of such amendment, no further action shall be taken on such petition. If a majority of such voters votes approval of such amendment, it shall become a part of this constitution upon completion of the canvass of votes by the supreme court.

Since the amendment of Article 19 in 1962, initiatives that propose constitutional amendments, as opposed to statutes, do not go to the legislature. That amendment requires them to be put on the ballot, after appropriate publication by the secretary of state, and they must be approved in two successive general elections to be enacted. Failure to pass either election by a simple majority of those voting on the question defeats the proposed amendment.

Amendments are considered adopted upon the official canvass of votes by the Nevada Supreme Court.

Sec: 3. Referendum and initiative petitions: Contents and form; signatures; enacting clause; manner of verification of signatures

1. Each referendum petition and initiative petition shall include the full text of the measure proposed. Each signer shall affix thereto his or her signature, residence address, and the name of the county in which he or she is a registered voter. The petition may consist of more than one document, but each document shall have affixed thereto an affidavit made by one of the signers of such document to the effect that all of the signatures are genuine and that each individual who signed such document was at the time of the signing a registered voter in the county of his or her residence. The affidavit shall be executed before a person authorized by law to administer oaths in the State of Nevada. The enacting clause of all statutes or amendments proposed by initiative petition shall be: "The People of the State of Nevada do enact as follows:".

2. The legislature may authorize the secretary of state and the other public officers to use generally accepted statistical procedures in conducting a preliminary verification of the numbers of signatures submitted in connection with a referendum petition or an initiative petition, and for this purpose to require petitions to be filed no more than 65 days earlier than is otherwise required by this article.

This section establishes the procedural rules for both referendum and initiative petitions, rules that "demand strict adherence" (*Lundberg v. Koontz*). Failure to adhere to these rules strictly is cause for the petitions to be rendered void. The courts have held petitions invalid that did not properly authenticate signatures

(*Lundberg v. Koontz*), did not include verbatim the enacting clause required by paragraph 1 (*Caine v. Robbins*), were circulated by individuals not registered to vote at the time of circulation (*Stumpf v. Lau*), and did not indicate whether the initiative was to be a proposed law, proposed constitutional amendment, or straw poll (*Stumpf v. Lau*).

Once a petition has been filed, the signer may not withdraw his or her name from the petition (Attorney General's Opinion 379, July 14, 1930).

Paragraph 2, added by amendment in 1988, allows the legislature to authorize verification of signatures by statistically drawing samples of signatures for authentication. The verifying officer thus does not have to engage in the costly and time-consuming process of validating every signature prior to deciding the validity of a petition.

Sec: 4. Powers of initiative and referendum of registered voters of counties and municipalities

> The initiative and referendum powers provided for in this article are further reserved to the registered voters of each county or each municipality as to all local, special and municipal legislation of every kind in or for such county or municipality. In counties and municipalities initiative petitions may be instituted by a number of registered voters equal to 15 percent or more of the voters who voted at the last preceding general county or municipal election. Referendum petitions may be instituted by 10 percent or more of such voters.

Section 4 was added in 1962 in part as a result of a supreme court decision that referendum and initiative as provided by Article 19 applied only to submission to the voters of the state and not to a county (*State ex rel. Dotta v. Brodigan*). This section extends these two processes to voters in counties and municipalities within the state with a slightly different signature requirement for initiative petitions. As with the state referendum process, only "legislative" and not "administrative" matters may be referred to the voters of a county or municipality (*Forman v. Eagle Thrifty Drugs & Markets, Inc.*).

County or municipal initiative petitions proposing legislation that would be unconstitutional if enacted do not have to be submitted to the voters by the city council or board of county commissioners (Attorney General's Opinion 79-3, February 13, 1979).

Sec: 5. Provisions of article self-executing; legislative procedures

> The provisions of this article are self-executing but the legislature may provide by law for procedures to facilitate the operation thereof.

This section, added in 1962, has not been subject to interpretation.

Sec: 6. **Limitation on initiative making appropriation or requiring expenditure of money**

This article does not permit the proposal of any statute or statutory amendment which makes an appropriation or otherwise requires the expenditure
of money, unless such statute or amendment also imposes a sufficient tax,
not prohibited by the constitution, or otherwise constitutionally provides for
raising the necessary revenue.

Section 6, added in 1972, has not been subject to interpretation.

Election Ordinance

The Election Ordinance contains rules and regulations governing the September 1864 election for ratification of the constitution and the November 1864 election for the state's first officers. In the sole case invoking these provisions, the Nevada Supreme Court held that the election ordinance applied only to these two elections mandated by the enabling act and not to any elections that might take place in the future (*State ex rel. McMillan v. Sadler*). Because these provisions are of historical interest only and are self-explanatory, they are provided here without section-by-section analysis or comment.

WHEREAS, The enabling act passed by Congress and approved March Twenty first A.D. Eighteen Hundred and Sixty four, requires that the convention charged with the duty of framing a Constitution for a State Government "shall provide by ordinance for submitting said Constitution to the People of the Territory of Nevada, for their ratification or rejection" on a certain day prescribed therein; therefore this Convention organized in pursuance of said enabling act, do establish the following:

ORDINANCE

Sec: 1. Proclamation by territorial governor; general election

The Governor of the Territory of Nevada is hereby authorized to issue his proclamation for the submission of this constitution to the people of said Territory for their approval or rejection on the day provided for such submission, by Act of Congress; and this Constitution shall be submitted to the qualified electors of said Territory, in the several counties thereof, for their approval or rejection, at the time provided by such Act of Congress; and further, on the first Tuesday after the first Monday of November A.D. Eighteen hundred and Sixty four, there shall be a general election in the several counties of said Territory for the election of State Officers, Supreme and District Judges, members of the Legislature, Representative in Congress and three Presidential Electors.

Sec: 2. Qualified electors may vote for adoption or rejection of constitution

All persons qualified by the laws of said Territory to vote for Representatives to the General Assembly on the said Twenty first day of March, including those in the Army of the United States, both within and beyond the boundaries of said Territory, and also all persons who may by the aforesaid laws, be qualified to vote on the first Wednesday of September A.D. Eighteen hundred and Sixty four, including those in the aforesaid Army of the United States, within and without the boundaries of said Territory may vote for the adoption or rejection of said Constitution, on the day last above named. In voting upon this Constitution, such elector shall deposite [sic] in the ballot box a ticket whereon shall be clearly written, or printed "Constitution Yes" or "Constitution No," or other such words that shall clearly indicate the intention of the Elector.

Sec: 3. Qualified electors for first general election

All persons qualified by the laws of said Territory to vote on the Tuesday after the first Monday of November A.D. Eighteen hundred and Sixty four, including those in the Army of the United States, within and beyond the boundaries of said Territory, may vote on the day last above named, for State Officers, Supreme and District Judges, Members of the Legislature, Representative in Congress, and three Presidential electors, to the electoral college.

Sec: 4. Elections: Places, judges, inspectors and procedures

The elections provided in this Ordinance shall be holden [sic] at such places as shall be designated by the Boards of Commissioners of the several counties in said Territory. The Judges, and inspectors of said elections, shall be appointed by said Commissioners, and the said elections shall be conducted in conformity with the existing laws of said Territory in relation to holding the General election.

Sec: 5. Election returns

The Judges and Inspectors of said elections shall carefully count each ballot immediately after said elections, and forthwith make duplicate returns thereof to the clerks of the said County Commissioners of their respective Counties, and said Clerks, within fifteen days after said elections shall transmit an abstract of the votes including the soldiers vote, as herein provided, given for State Officers, Supreme and District Judges, Representative in Congress and three Presidential Electors, enclosed in an envelope, by the most safe and expeditious conveyance to the Governor of said Territory marked "Election Returns."

Sec: 6. Canvass of votes; proclamation; issuance of certificates of election

Upon the receipt of said returns, including those of the soldiers vote, or within Twenty days after the election, if said returns be not sooner received, it shall be the duty of the Board of Canvassers, to consist of the Governor, United States District Attorney and Chief Justice of said Territory or any two of them to canvass the returns in the presence of all who may wish to be present, and if a majority of all the votes given upon this Constitution, shall be in its favor, the said Governor shall immediately publish an abstract of the same, and make proclamation of the fact in some newspaper in said Territory and certify the same to the President of the United States, together with a copy of the Constitution and Ordinance. The said Board of Canvassers, after canvassing the votes of the said November elections shall issue certificates of election, to such persons as were elected State Officers, Judges of the Supreme and District Courts, Representative in Congress and three Presidential Electors. When the President of the United States shall issue his proclamation, declaring this State admitted into the Union, on an equal footing, with the original states; This Constitution shall thenceforth be ordained and established as the Constitution of the State of Nevada.

Sec: 7. List of electors in Army of the United States

For the purpose of taking the vote of the Electors of said Territory who may be in the Army of the United States: the Adjutant General of said Territory, shall on or before the fifth day of August next following, make out a list in alphabetical order and deliver same to the Governor, of the names of all electors, residents of said Territory, who shall be in the Army of the United States, stating the number of the Regiment, Battalion, Squadron, or Battery, to which he belongs, and also the County or Township, of his residence in said Territory.

Sec: 8. Transmission of lists of electors in Army of the United States

The Governor shall classify and arrange the aforesaid list, and shall make therefrom separate lists of the electors belonging to each Reigment [sic],

Battalion, Squadron and Battery from said Territory in the Service of the United States, and shall, on or before the Fifteenth day of August following, transmit by mail or otherwise, to the Commanding Officer of each Regiment, Battalion, Squadron and Battery, a list of electors belonging thereto, which said list shall specify the name, residence and rank of each elector, and the company to which he belongs, if to any, and also the County and Township to which he belongs, and in which he is entitled to vote.

Sec: 9. **Voting by soldiers: Qualifications**

Between the hours of Nine O'Clock A.M. and Three O'Clock P.M. on each of the election days hereinbefore named, a ballot box or suitable receptacle for votes shall be opened under the immediate charge and direction of three of the highest Officers in command, for the reception of Votes from the electors whose names are upon said list, at each place where a Regiment, Battalion, Squadron or Battery of Soldiers from said Territory in the Army of the United States may be on that day; at which time and place, said Electors shall be entitled to vote for all Officers for which by reason of their residence in the several counties in said Territory they are authorized to vote, as fully as they would be entitled to vote in the several Counties or Townships in which they reside, and the votes so given by such electors at such time and place, shall be considered, taken and held to have been given by them in the respective Counties and Townships in which they are resident.

Sec: 10. **Voting by soldiers: Procedure; count of votes**

Each ballot deposited for the adoption or rejection of this Constitution, in the Army of the United States shall have, distinctly written or printed thereon "Constitution Yes", or "Constitution No"; or words of a similar import, and further, for the election of State Officers, Supreme and District Judges, Members of the Legislature, Representative in Congress and three Presidential Electors, the name and Office of the person voted for shall be plainly written or printed on one piece of paper. The name of each elector voting as aforesaid shall be checked upon the said list, at the time of voting by one of the said Officers, having charge of the ballot box. The said Officers having charge of the election shall count the votes and compare them with the checked list, immediately after the closing of the ballot box.

Sec: 11. **Voting by soldiers: Transmission of results**

All the ballots case, together with the said voting list, checked as aforesaid, shall be immediately sealed up, and sent forthwith to the Governor of said Territory at Carson City by mail or otherwise, by the Commanding Officer, who shall make out and certify duplicate returns of Votes given, according to the forms hereinafter prescribed, seal up and immediately transmit the same to the said Governor at Carson City by mail or otherwise, the day following the transmission of the ballots and the voting list herein named, the said Commanding Officer shall also immediately transmit to the several County Clerks in said Territory an abstract of the votes given at the general election in November, for County Officers marked "Election Returns".

Sec: 12. **Voting by soldiers: Form of return**

The form of returns of votes to be made by the Commanding Officer to the Governor and County Clerks of said Territory shall be in substance as follows, Viz: "Returns of Soldiers, votes in the (here insert the regiment, detachment, battalion, squadron or battery)"—(For first election on the Constitution.) _____ I _____ hereby certify, that, on the first Wednesday of September A.D. Eighteen hundred and sixty four the Electors belonging to the (here insert the name of the regiment, detachment, battalion, squadron or battery.) cast the following number of votes for and against the Constitution for the State of Nevada, Viz: For "Constitution" (number of votes written in full and in figures.) Against "Constitution" (number of votes written in full and in figures) _____ (Second election for State and other Officers) _____ I _____ hereby certify that on the first Tuesday after the first Monday in November A.D. Eighteen hundred and Sixty four, the Electors belonging to the (here insert as above) cast the following number of votes for the several officers and persons hereinafter named Viz: _____ For Governor _____ names of persons voted for written in full and also in figures, against the name of each person. _____ For Lieutenant Governor _____ name of Candidates, number of votes cast for each, written out and in figures as above. _____ Continue as above till the list is completed _____

_____ Attest _____   I, A.B. _____

_____ _____   Commanding Officer of the

_____ _____   (here Insert regiment, detachment, battalion, squadron, or battery as the case may be).

Sec: 13. **Voting by soldiers: Territorial governor to furnish form of return**

The Governor of this Territory is requested to furnish each Commanding Officer within and beyond the boundaries of said Territory, proper and sufficient blanks for said returns.

Sec: 14. **Applicability to future votes of soldiers**

The provisions of this Ordinance in regard to the Soldiers vote shall apply to future elections under this Constitution, and be in full force until the

Legislature shall provide by law for taking the votes of citizens of said Territory in the Army of the United States.

DONE IN CONVENTION, at Carson City the Twenty Eighth day of July, in the year of our Lord One Thousand Eight Hundred and Sixty Four and of the Independence of the United States the Eighty-ninth, and signed by the Delegates.
[Then follow the names of delegates who signed the constitution.]

Notes

1. In this sense, the Nevada Constitution's Ordinance is similar to Article V of the U.S. Constitution, which prohibits amending that document to deprive a state of "its equal Suffrage in the Senate" without its consent. That provision, like Nevada's, has not been challenged in the courts, and there are reputable arguments on both sides of the question as to whether it is unamendable. See J. W. Peltason, *Understanding the Constitution*, 11th ed. (New York: Holt, Rinehart and Winston, 1988), 124. Furthermore, the U.S. Supreme Court held in *Coyle v. Smith* that although the federal government may establish certain preconditions to statehood, once an area becomes a state, it is on an equal footing with other states and cannot be denied the rights possessed by other states to change its constitution (so long as these changes are not violative of the federal constitution).

2. The five that have not been applied to the states are the Second Amendment, the Third Amendment, the grand jury clause of the Fifth Amendment, the Seventh Amendment, and the excessive fines and bails clause of the Eighth Amendment. For an excellent examination of the incorporation process, see Richard C. Cortner, *The Supreme Court and the Second Bill of Rights: The Fourteenth Amendment and the Nationalization of Civil Liberties* (Madison: University of Wisconsin Press, 1981).

3. See, for example, Hans A. Linde, "First Things First: Rediscovering the States' Bills of Rights," *University of Baltimore Law Review* 9 (1980), 379.

4. Andrew J. Marsh, Official Reporter, *Official Report of the Debates and Proceedings in the Constitutional Convention of the State of Nevada* (San Francisco: Frank Eastman, 1866), 59.

5. Gordon Morris Bakken, *Rocky Mountain Constitution Making, 1850–1912* (Westport, Conn.: Greenwood Press, 1987), 26.

6. Jay M. Shafritz, *The Dorsey Dictionary of American Government and Politics* (Chicago: Dorsey Press, 1988), 244.

7. Marsh, *Debates and Proceedings*, 194–96.

8. Marsh, *Debates and Proceedings*, 786.

9. David Alan Johnson, *Founding the Far West: California, Oregon, and Nevada, 1840–1890* (Berkeley: University of California Press, 1992), 213.

10. Ibid., 229.

11. Marsh, *Debates and Proceedings*, 144.

12. Ibid., 154.

13. Ibid., 159.

14. Eleanore Bushnell and Don W. Driggs, *The Nevada Constitution: Origin and Growth*, 6th ed. (Reno: University of Nevada Press, 1984), 97–98.

15. Marsh, *Debates and Proceedings*, 642.

16. Lawrence Baum, *American Courts: Process and Policy*, 2d ed. (Boston: Houghton Mifflin, 1990), 101.

17. Michael W. Bowers, "The Impact of Judicial Selection Methods in Nevada: Some Empirical Observations," *Nevada Public Affairs Review*, no. 2 (1990), 3–8.

18. On the issue of replacement of supreme court justices for disability or disqualification, see Barnett and Rubinfeld, "The Assignment of Temporary Justices in the California Supreme Court," *Pacific Law Journal* 17 (1986), 1045.

19. See A. Constandina Titus, "Toward a Consolidated Approach to Legally-Related Domestic Problems: Nevada Creates a Family Court," *Nevada Public Affairs Review*, no. 2 (1990), 18–22.

20. The actions leading up to the adoption of Rule 7 are examined in Michael W. Bowers, "Personality and Judicial Politics in Nevada," *State Constitutional Commentaries and Notes* 2, no. 4 (Summer 1991), 7–10.

21. Harry P. Stumpf, *American Judicial Politics* (San Diego: Harcourt Brace Jovanovich, 1988), 168.

22. The modified merit system adopted in Nevada and the restrictions upon it are discussed in Michael W. Bowers, "Judicial Selection in Nevada: Choosing the Judges," *Halcyon 1989: A Journal of the Humanities* 11 (1989), 97–98.

23. For an examination of the merit system from a participant observer who once sat on the Nevada Supreme Court, see E. M. Gunderson, " 'Merits Selection': The Report and Appraisal of a Participant Observer," *Pacific Law Journal* 10 (1979), 683.

24. See Marsh, *Debates and Proceedings*, 541.

25. Bakken, *Rocky Mountain Constitution Making*, 40. For the convention debate on this issue, see Marsh, *Debates and Proceedings*, 544–65.

26. Marsh, *Debates and Proceedings*, 164.

27. Bakken, *Rocky Mountain Constitution Making*, 66.

28. Bushnell and Driggs, *Nevada Constitution*, 45.

29. See Michael W. Bowers, "Federal Term Limits and the Nevada Supreme Court," *State Constitutional Commentaries and Notes* 3, no. 3 (Spring 1992).

Bibliographical Essay

There are a number of useful general bibliographies on Nevada history and politics. Russell R. Elliott and Helen J. Poulton, *Writings on Nevada: A Selected Bibliography* (Reno: University of Nevada Press, 1963), is an excellent and comprehensive source for materials written before 1963. More recent listings of sources can be found in the appendixes of James W. Hulse, *The Silver State: Nevada's Heritage Reinterpreted* (Reno and Las Vegas: University of Nevada Press, 1991), and Russell R. Elliott with William D. Rowley, *History of Nevada*, 2d ed., rev. (Lincoln: University of Nebraska Press, 1987).

A wealth of material on Nevada's history, politics, and culture can be found by examining the many volumes and indexes of *Nevada Historical Society Quarterly, Nevada Public Affairs Review, and Halcyon: A Journal of the Humanities*. All three of these scholarly journals frequently publish articles on various Nevada topics.

NEVADA HISTORY

The many volumes on Nevada history are varied in their merit and contemporaneity. Some of the classic, but dated, works are Myron Angel (ed.), *History of Nevada, 1881, with Illustrations* (Oakland, Calif.: Thompson and West, 1881; reissued by Berkeley: Howell-North, 1958); Hubert Howe Bancroft, *The Works of Hubert Howe Bancroft*, Vol. 15: *History of Nevada, Colorado, and Wyoming: 1540–1888* (San Francisco: History Co., Publ.; reprinted by Reno: University of Nevada Press, 1981); Samuel P. Davis (ed.), *The History of Nevada*, 2 vols. (Reno, Los Angeles: Elms Publishing Co., 1913); Richard G. Lillard, *Desert Challenge: An Interpretation of Nevada* (New York: Alfred A. Knopf, 1942); and Effie Mona Mack, *Nevada: A History of the State from the Earliest Times through the Civil War* (Glendale, Calif.: Arthur H. Clark, 1936).

More recent histories can be found in Elliott, *History of Nevada*, and Hulse, *The Silver State*, cited above, and James W. Hulse, *The Nevada Adventure: A History*, 6th ed. (Reno and Las Vegas: University of Nevada Press, 1990). Critical analyses of Nevada's history, politics, and culture are found in Gilman M. Ostrander, *Nevada: The Great Rotten Borough, 1859–1964* (New York: Alfred A. Knopf, 1966), and James W. Hulse, *Forty Years in the Wilderness: Impressions of Nevada, 1940–1980* (Reno: University of Nevada Press, 1986).

NEVADA GOVERNMENT AND POLITICS

Much less has been written on Nevada politics and government than on the state's history. Two good, but dated, texts will give the reader a general sense of Nevada government: Albert C. Johns, *Nevada Politics* (Dubuque, Iowa: Kendall/Hunt Publ. Co., 1973), and Effie Mona Mack, Idel Anderson, and Beulah E. Singleton, *Nevada Government: A Study of the Administration and Politics of State, County, Township, and Cities* (Caldwell, Idaho: Caxton Printers, 1953).

A more recent, but still dated, work on Nevada government and politics is Eleanore Bushnell and Don W. Driggs, *The Nevada Constitution: Origin and Growth*, 6th ed. (Reno: University of Nevada Press, 1984). Also somewhat dated but still quite useful is a chapter on Nevada politics by Eleanore Bushnell in Frank H. Jonas (ed.), *Politics in the American West* (Salt Lake City: University of Utah Press, 1969). The most current summary of Nevada's government can be found in Michael W. Bowers and Timothy Haller, "Primer on Nevada Government," in *Battle Born: Federal-State Conflict in Nevada during the Twentieth Century*, ed. A. Constandina Titus (Dubuque, Iowa: Kendall/Hunt Publ. Co., 1989).

An excellent overview of Nevada in comparison with other western politics and governments can be found in Clive S. Thomas (ed.), *Politics and Public Policy in the Contemporary American West* (Albuquerque: University of New Mexico Press, 1991).

Frankie Sue Del Papa (Secretary of State), *Political History of Nevada: 1990* (Carson City: State Printing Office, 1990), is extremely useful as a reference work on early Nevada history, election returns, the state's boundary, and the state's elected officers.

The politics of apportionment and reapportionment is dealt with in Eleanore Bushnell (ed.), *Impact of Reapportionment on the Thirteen Western States* (Salt Lake City: University of Utah Press, 1970); Eleanore Bushnell, "Reapportionment and Responsibility," in *Sagebrush and Neon: Studies in Nevada Politics*," ed. Eleanore Bushnell (Reno: Bureau of Governmental Research, 1976); and Don W. Driggs, "Legislative Apportionment," *Governmental Research Newsletter* 1, no. 4 (January 1961).

Minority politics in Nevada have been covered extensively in several articles in Elmer R. Rusco and Sue Fawn Chung (eds.), "Ethnicity and Race in Nevada," *Nevada Public Affairs Review*, no. 2 (1987). Among the topics included in that volume are African-Americans (Roosevelt Fitzgerald) and Hispanics (M. L. Miranda). Additional sources to consult are Elmer R. Rusco, *"Good Time Coming?" Black Nevadans in the Nineteenth Century* (Westport, Conn.: Greenwood Press, 1975); Elmer R. Rusco, *Minority Groups in Nevada* (Reno: Bureau of Government Research, 1966); and Joseph N. Crowley, "Race and Residence: The Politics of Open Housing in Nevada," in *Sagebrush and Neon: Studies in Nevada Politics*, ed. Eleanore Bushnell (Reno: Bureau of Government Research, 1976).

Discrimination against the Chinese is covered in Sue Fawn Chung, "The Chinese Experience in Nevada: Success Despite Discrimination," *Nevada Public Affairs Review*, no. 2 (1987), and Russell M. Magnaghi, "Virginia City's Chinese Community, 1860–1880," *Nevada Historical Society Quarterly* 24 (Summer 1981).

For a biography of the leading feminist in pioneer Nevada, see Anne Bail Howard, *The Long Campaign: A Biography of Anne Martin* (Reno: University of Nevada Press, 1985).

NEVADA CONSTITUTIONS AND CONVENTIONS

The best source on the 1863 constitutional convention remains William C. Miller and Eleanore Bushnell (eds.), *Reports of the 1863 Constitutional Convention of the Territory of Nevada* (Carson City: Legislative Counsel Bureau, 1972). The notes of the 1864 convention are preserved in Andrew J. Marsh, *Official Report of the Debates and Proceedings in the Constitutional Convention of the State of Nevada* (San Francisco: Frank Eastman, 1866).

The important role of William M. Stewart in the state's constitution-making process is discussed in Russell R. Elliott, *Servant of Power: A Political Biography of Senator William M. Stewart* (Reno: University of Nevada Press, 1983), and David A. Johnson, "A Case of Mistaken Identity: William M. Stewart and the Rejection of Nevada's First Constitution," *Nevada Historical Society Quarterly* 22 (Fall 1979). The pivotal role played at the 1864 convention by four other delegates (Collins, Johnson, Fitch, and DeLong) is examined in David A. Johnson, *Founding the Far West: California, Oregon, and Nevada: 1840–1890* (Berkeley: University of California Press, 1992).

Gordon Morris Bakken, *Rocky Mountain Constitution Making, 1850–1912* (Westport, Conn.: Greenwood Press, 1987), places the Nevada convention and constitution within the context of other state conventions and constitutions in the Rocky Mountains during that period.

Little has been written and published on the topic of the Nevada Constitution itself. A dated, but still helpful, work is Don W. Driggs, *The Constitution of the State of Nevada: A Commentary* (Carson City: State Printing Office, 1961). The convention and some of the major debates within it are discussed in Eleanore Bushnell and Don Driggs (eds.), *The Nevada Constitution: Origin and Growth*, noted above.

Nevada does not have a law school or law review, and, therefore, the literature on Nevada constitutional interpretation is sparse. The *Nevada Lawyer* (formerly titled *Inter Alia*), published by the Nevada Bar Association, publishes that type of material, as do some of the California law reviews. Most relevant are the many volumes of the *Southwestern University Law Journal*, *Pacific Law Journal*, *Western State University Law Review*, and *Whittier Law Review*.

Research of a particular constitutional provision is best accomplished by examining the annotations in the first volume of *Nevada Revised Statutes Annotated* (St. Paul, Minn.: West Publishing Company) and then reading the cases themselves in the *Nevada Reports* or the *Pacific Reporter*.

Table of Cases

Index

About the Author

MICHAEL W. BOWERS is Associate Dean of the College of Liberal Arts and Associate Professor of Political Science at the University of Nevada at Las Vegas. He specializes in public law, judicial selection, and Nevada politics and has written and published at length on these subjects.